the best of british illustration

images
22

Images 22 published by Rotovision SA
7 Rue du Bugnon
CH – 1299 Crans
Switzerland

Project Manager: Alexandra Oke
Telephone: 0171 831 7977

Book Design: Nicole Griffin

Administrator: Stephanie Smith

Production in Singapore by Provision
Pty Ltd
Telephone: +65 334 7720
Fax: +65 334 7721

Rotovision SA
Editorial & Sales Office
Sheridan House
112/116A Western Road
Hove BN3 1DD
England
Tel: +44 1273 72 72 68
Fax: +44 1273 72 72 69

Association of Illustrators
1st Floor, 32/38 Saffron Hill
London EC1N 8FH
Tel: +44 171 831 7377
Fax: +44 171 831 6277

Acknowledgements
- Our 40 judges on the judging panel for applying their expertise to the difficult task of selecting this year's work
- The Royal College of Art for hosting the *Images 22* exhibition
- Moshe Gerstenhaber and Nigel Toplis at Kall Kwik for sponsoring the AOI/Kall Kwik Illustrator Award and Kall Kwik Print and Design Award, and for their boundless support for British Illustration
- Waterstone's Booksellers, Pentagram, Windsor and Newton and Daler-Rowney for their generosity in sponsoring awards for *Images 22*
- Brian Grimwood for the use of his illustrations on both the Call for Entry form and various press releases, and for interviewing the winners of the AOI/Kall Kwik Illustrator Award
- Ruth Gladwin and Sarah Davis of Stephens Innocent Solicitors
- Stephens Innocent Solicitors who continue to support the AOI and the rights of illustrators
- All our volunteers whose invaluable and professional assistance for the competition, annual and exhibition allows the AOI to operate at its current high level
- AOI Managing Council: Stuart Briers (Chair), Francis Blake, Lee Beech, Michael Bramman, Derek Brazell, Andrew Bylo, Ruth Gladwin, Adam Graff, Geoff Grandfield, Pauline Hazelwood, Fern Warshell, James Marsh, Bee Willey and Margaret Wellbank

Credits
Illustrations of Judges:
Advertising:
 Adam Graff (0181 509 1489)
Children's Books:
 Adam Graff
Editorial:
 Peter Clark (0181 979 4593)
General Books:
 Peter Clark
Information:
 Claire Pettinati (01273 674448)
Print and Design:
 Andrew Bylo (0171 274 4116)
Student:
 Jake Abrams (0181 255 9828/
 0956 516216)
Unpublished:
 Bee Willey (0171 375 0323)

Contents

Foreword

by Stuart Briers / AOI Chairman

Welcome to *Images 22*

The Association of Illustrators is pleased to present our latest annual, featuring close to 200 pages of leading illustration. With its distribution of 8,000 in the UK and 6,000 worldwide, *Images* will now be seen by more commissioners of illustration than ever before, giving British illustration the showcase it truly deserves.

Images and I go back a long way – to the third annual to be exact. I had just left college in the late 70's, and caught sight of the sumptuous 'panda' cover illustration by Peter Brookes in a bookshop. On further inspection the contents of the book were no less impressive. In those days collections of illustration were extremely thin on the ground and to a fledgling illustrator such as myself the book was nothing short of revelatory. The quality and diversity of the work on display provided me with a much-needed focus.

This initial impression was further cemented in the ensuing years as *Images* went from strength to strength with its heady mix of innovation and craftsmanship. By the mid/late 80's the book had earned itself an enviable reputation and was perceived throughout the industry as representing a benchmark of quality.

As well as being a continuing source of inspiration for illustrators, *Images* has helped to create a demand for illustration and influenced commissioners in the type of work they can use.

Today the illustration landscape has considerably altered. The advent of new technology has blurred the dividing lines which have traditionally separated photography from illustration and graphics to the degree where defining what illustration actually is becomes a rather difficult, and perhaps pointless excercise. My own view (that regardless of tool or technique, illustration is drawing based) would omit, for example, collage works and virtually all current computer-generated work. The dictionary, however, provides us with a more adequate definition – 'illustrator' derives from the Latin 'lustrare': to light up. An illustration therefore is a picture that illuminates. I hope you are as illuminated in your perusal of *Images 22* as I was twenty-odd years ago when confronted with the Peter Brookes panda.

***Images 22* tour**

Tour venues will include:
• University of Brighton Gallery, Brighton • St. David's Hall, Cardiff • Collins Gallery, Glasgow • European Illustration Collection, Hull • Derby Museum and Art Gallery, Derby

Introduction to the AOI

The AOI was established in 1973 to advance and protect illustrators' rights and encourage professional standards. The AOI is a non-profit making trade association dedicated to its members' professional interests and the promotion of illustration.

Members consist primarily of freelance illustrators as well as agents, clients, students and lecturers. The AOI has its offices at the Chartered Society of Designers in Central London and is run by an administrative staff responsible to a Council of Management, made up of illustrators elected at the Annual General Meeting.

During its history, the AOI has been the only body to represent illustrators and campaign for their rights in the UK. It has successfully increased the standing of illustration as a profession and improved the commercial and ethical conditions of employment for illustrators.

Campaigning

As part of its campaigning role the AOI is a member of the British Copyright Council and was instrumental in setting up JECVA (Joint Ethics Committee for the Visual Arts).

It is a member of the Industry Lead Body for Design, the Arts and Entertainment Training Council and the Design and Artists Copyright Society (DACS).

The AOI was responsible for establishing the right of illustrators to retain ownership of their artwork and continues to campaign against loss of copyright control, bad contracts and exploitative practices. We will expose companies who consistently abuse illustrators' rights.

Portfolio advice

Members are entitled to a free annual consultation with the AOI's professional portfolio consultant. Objective advice is given on portfolio presentation and content, suitable illustration markets and agents.

Journal

The AOI Journal *Illustrator* is distributed monthly to members, keeping them informed about exhibitions, competitions, campaigns and activities in the profession.

Hotline advice

Members have access to a special Hotline number if they need advice about pricing commissions, copyright and ethics problems.

Publications

The AOI publishes *Rights* (*The Illustrator's Guide to Professional Practice*), a comprehensive guide to the law for illustrators. It provides detailed advice on the illustrator's legal position, protection against exploitative practices and contains a model contract for illustrators to use. We also produce *Survive* (*The Illustrator's Guide to a Professional Career*) which is a comprehensive practical guide to beginning and continuing a career as a professional illustrator. *Survive* includes information about marketing, ethics, agents and a guide to fees. These publications are available to members at reduced rates.

Client directories

The AOI currently has two illustration client directories which are only available for purchase by members. The *Editorial Directory* has details of over 120 contacts in the newspaper and magazine industries. The *Publishing Directory* is a comprehensive list of important contacts in book publishing.

Business advice

Members are entitled to a free consultation with the AOI Chartered Accountant, who can advise on accounting, National Insurance, tax, VAT and book-keeping.

Regional groups

The contact details of regional representatives are available to members who organise social activities for regional members and provide an important support network.

Discounts

Discounts on selected hotel accommodation in London, photographic services, courier services, printers and art material suppliers nationwide.

Portfolio insurance

The AOI has a portfolio insurance scheme designed specifically and exclusively for its members.

Central London meeting place

Regional members may use the AOI offices for meetings with clients.

Return of artwork stickers

Available to AOI members only. These stickers help safeguard the return of artwork.

Students and new illustrators

The AOI organises programmes of seminars and workshops on professional practice specifically for students and new illustrators.

Image file

Members can promote their work to clients visiting the AOI office via the *Image File* containing copies of members' work.

Events

The AOI runs an annual programme of events which include one-day seminars, thematic exhibitions, evening lectures, forums and workshops, covering subjects such as talks by leading illustrators, children's book illustration, aspects of professional practice, new technologies and illustrators' agents. AOI members have priority booking and are entitled to discounted tickets.

ASSOCIATION OF ILLUSTRATORS

AOI

RONALD SEARLE

IAN POLLOCK

Ronald Searle

Ronald Searle, born Cambridge 1920, began freelancing almost immediately and is still at it. Has contributed to the *New Yorker* Magazine on and off since 1966 and, more recently, has become an editorial cartoonist to the French newspaper *Le Monde*.

Ian Pollock

Pollock has worked as a freelance illustrator since graduating from the Royal College of Art in 1976 – 'Busy ever since,' he says. He works mostly for magazines and newspapers and appears regularly in the 'quality press.'

He was recently commissioned to design four postage stamps – 'Tales of Terror' – for The Royal Mail which were issued in May 1997.

Pollock, now in remission, lives in a weaver's cottage in Macclesfield with his understanding wife and two children.

Chloe Cheese

I left the R.C.A. in 1976 and work as an illustrator and printmaker. I have exhibitions of my paintings and prints. To work as a freelance illustrator is a pleasure; it is a voyage of discovery starting, for me, with patisserie in Paris and at the moment alighting at children's books and teaching illustration in Beirut.

CHLOE CHEESE

BRIAN GRIMWOOD

Brian Grimwood

Brian Grimwood has been credited by *Print* magazine as having changed the look of British illustration. He has worked for most of the major publications in the UK and Europe, and has become one of Britain's most innovative and influential illustrators.

In 1983 he co-founded the Central Illustration Agency that now represents 50 of London's most prestigious illustrators.

As well as exhibiting in numerous group shows, he has had four 'one-man exhibitions'. The most recent was at the Portland Gallery, St James, London.

GLEN BAXTER

Glen Baxter

Glen Baxter was born in the tiny Northern hamlet of Hunslet. After a series of educational errors he was removed and installed in a crumbling Victorian manor house in Camberwell, where his condition is said to be 'almost stable.'

He is the author of *The Impending Gleam*, *Cranireons ov Botya*, *The Wonder Book of Sex* and *Glen Baxter's Gourmet Guide*.

His drawings have been exhibited in Paris, New York, Venice, Tokyo, Sydney, Amsterdam and Ikley.

He is currently working on a hydraulic device for the removal of unsightly gussets.

Simon Stern

Simon Stern was born in 1943, studied graphic design at the London College of Printing and worked as a designer for some years before turning to writing and illustrating children's books and later to general illustration. He has made a special study of the legal issues associated with illustration, and wrote the AOI publication. He has been associated with the AOI since 1975.

SIMON STERN

Shirley Hughes

Shirley Hughes has freelanced as an illustrator since the 1950's and worked on a great many books by other authors before she began to write and design her own picture books. One of these, *Dogger*, won the 1977 Kate Greenaway medal and in 1984 she was presented with the Eleanor Farjeon Award for services to children's literature. Her books, particularly the *Alfie* series, are in co-edition worldwide.

SHIRLEY HUGHES

Night Flight

Annie flew out of the window,
Bedclothes and cot and all,
And floated around above the ground,
And over the garden wall.

And her shadow skimmed over the gardens
And followed her all the way,
As she looked down on the roofs of the town
And the moon shone as bright as day.

JANET WOOLLEY

RAYMOND BRIGGS

TONY ROSS

Raymond Briggs

Raymond Briggs: born 1934. Painting student Wimbledon School of Art and Slade School. Illustrator since 1957. Writer since 1961. Best-known books: *Father Christmas* 1973, *Fungus the Bogeyman* 1977, *The Snowman* 1979, *When the Wind Blows* 1982 (book, radio play, stage play and feature film). More recently, *The Man and the Bear*. At present working on a strip cartoon biography of his parents called *Ethel and Earnest* to be published in 1997.

Janet Woolley

I left the R.C.A. in 1976, and have worked as an illustrator in Europe, UK and USA.

In 1991 having worked in a similar way for 15 years, I decided to make a change and started to work with montage. I continue to work in this way, taking more of my own photographs and painting them.

I am the resident Professor of Illustration at Central St Martins, where I have taught for 11 years.

Tony Ross

Born in London, lives and works with his family in Cheshire. Studied at Liverpool Art School, went on to work in graphic design and advertising, cartoon drawing and animated film. Also lectures.

Since 1983 has illustrated around 350 books and written about 70 (mainly published by Anderson Press in England, and others including Harper Collins).

Peter Blake

I am very proud to be the only artist who is both a Royal Academician as a painter and a Royal Designer to Industry as an illustrator.

PETER BLAKE

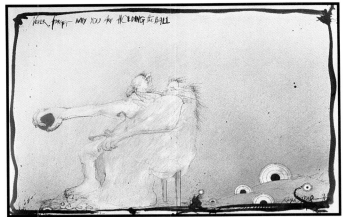

RALPH STEADMAN

Quentin Blake

Quentin Blake read English at Cambridge University, and Education at London University, before becoming a part-time student at Chelsea School of Art and a full-time freelance illustrator simultaneously, just about 40 years ago. He taught in the illustration department of the Royal College of Art, which he ran for several years. He finds drawing and the relationship of words and pictures unfailingly interesting.

Carolyn Gowdy

Carolyn Gowdy was born in Seattle, USA, studied at the University of Washington, Seattle, Rhode Island School of Design, Providence and the Royal College of Art, London.

Since 1977 she has lived in London and worked internationally as a painter and illustrator. She has also written and illustrated books for both children and adults.

'I'm a painter, illustrator, poet and writer. In my work I am particularly interested in researching the areas of personal identity and LIFE! For me it is a pleasure to explore the planet earth and to describe what I see, hear and feel along the way. I have an eye.'

Ralph Steadman

Ralph Steadman became a freelance cartoonist and illustrator after attending the London College of Printing and Graphic Arts in the early 1960's, working for *Punch*, *Private Eye*, *The Telegraph*, *New York Times* and *Rolling Stone* Magazine.

He has written and illustrated books on Sigmund Freud, Leonardo Da Vinci, *The Big I Am* (the story of creation and its aftermath), and *Tales of The Weird* (a collection of eccentrics and obsessive characters in history). He has illustrated *Alice in Wonderland*, *Alice Through The Looking Glass* and *The Hunting of The Snark, Treasure Island*, the works of Flann O'Brien and, most recently, the anniversary edition of *Animal Farm* in 1995.

Having travelled the world's vineyards and distilleries for Oddbins, he has illustrated and written two books of his journeys – *Grapes of Ralph* and *Still Life With Bottle*.

For the past few years he has been working on a series of etchings and silkscreen prints exploring the theme of 'leaders and writers' with Peacock Printmakers, Aberdeen. These works have been exhibited in Aberdeen, Denver and Aspen in the US.

In 1987, Ralph Steadman was the recipient of the W.H. Smith Illustration Award for the best illustrated book of the past five years (for *I Leonardo*) and the BBC Design Award for postage stamps. He also won the Italian Critica in Erba Prize and the Black Humour Award in France. He is a Fellow of the Kent Institute of Art and Design, and in 1995 was awarded an Hon.D.Litt. by the University of Kent.

CAROLYN GOWDY

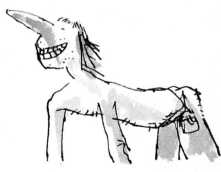

QUENTIN BLAKE

The AOI/Kall Kwik Illustrator Award

★ award winners: Tilly Northedge and Adrian Johnson

Interview by Brian Grimwood

To be successful, a good illustrator has to deliver a focused message using images which can be instantly identified and understood by the intended audience.

Good illustrations invariably exhibit imagination, creativity and wit, as well as the technical skills of the artist.

Kall Kwik is pleased to be associated with the AOI *Images 22* annual and exhibition and is very proud to be helping it to promote illustration excellence, imagination and creativity.

Walt Disney once said 'Disneyland will never be completed as long as there is imagination left in the world.' The work of the perceptive illustrator will never be completed either, as long as there are ideas which merit exposure or products left to sell.

Moshe Gerstenhaber

Chairman and Founder
Kall Kwik Printing (UK) Limited

Tilly Northedge is delighted that she has won such a focal award for her entry in the Information section. A passionate advocate of information illustration and design, Tilly hopes that the award will shed light on this 'Cinderella' area of illustration: the 'humble communication of information', which has never had a glamour tag attached.

After training as a graphic designer at Central St Martins, Tilly then went on to do an MA in Graphic Information at the Royal College of Art where she found herself drawing information pictures and moving into illustration. She also met and formed a partnership with fellow designer Peter Grundy. Grundy & Northedge has, for the past 17 years, aimed to make information more accessible, visually exciting and communicative, if not fun.

Clients include design groups, publishers, magazines and newspapers. Research is usually done by the client, but Tilly maintains that she has to understand the work in order to conceptualise and realise the project.

Tilly has moved from working in flat gouache with overlays to working almost exclusively with a computer, which has facilitated her style rather than changed it. Tilly has developed her own visual language and icons, but is wary of letting this hamper understanding of the information: content should not be diluted by style.

Tilly would like to move into animated diagrams and multimedia, as she feels information is moving away from print and into computer-based applications such as CD Roms and websites.

Adrian Johnson had just taken down his degree show the day that he learned he had won the award. He has since accepted his first commission from a children's book publisher.

A graduate from Kingston University, which encourages conceptualisation and an individual style, Adrian's early influences were his mother, an art teacher, and also the TV cartoons of the late 50's and early 60's, such as 'Mr Magoo' and 'The Pink Panther'. This inspired his current use of bold, vibrant, flat colour and abstract background. A trip to Spain and a love of Brazilian Salsa and Samba music sparked off a series of moustachioed Latinos, one of which features in *Tabasco, Sombrero Bandido*.

Adrian cheerfully admits that he is an illustrator as he is 'no good at anything else' and wants to make a career 'doing something I love while trying to avoid growing up for as long as possible . . .'

Reaction to his work is that Adrian is having fun (which caught the eye of the *Images* judges as well), and he aims to stamp his style 'all over' any commission.

His current illustration heroes are Benoit Jacques and Satoshi Kitamura.

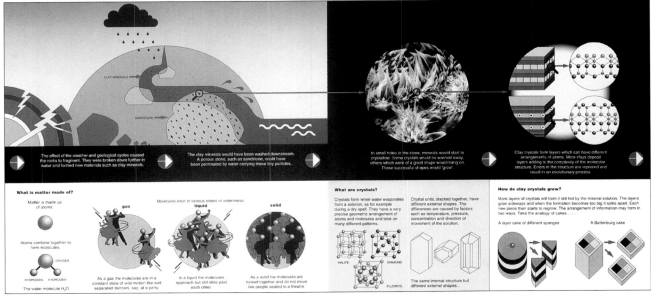

Images 22 award winners

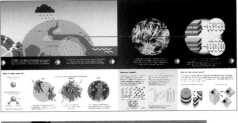

The AOI/Kall Kwik Illustrator Award

★ **award winner:** Tilly Northedge:
How Did Life Begin – 2
★ **award winner:** Adrian Johnson:
Tabasco, Sombrero, Bandido

£1000 and a free page, awarded to the illustrator with the maximum overall marks from the judging panel

The Kall Kwik Print & Design Award

★ **award winner:** Satoshi Kambayashi:
Summersault / July

£500 awarded to the highest-scoring illustration in the Print & Design section

The Client award

★ **award winner:** David Freeman, Sampson Tyrrell for *Understanding the Client Brief* by Bruce Ingman

£400, awarded to the commissioning editor who submitted illustrations which received the highest marks from the judging panel

W

WATERSTONE'S

Waterstone's Booksellers Award

★ **award winner:** Geoff Grandfield *Stamboul Train*

£500 of book vouchers for the illustration with the highest marks from the judging panel in the General Books section

The Transworld Children's Book Award

★ **award winner:** Andrew Davidson *Godhanger*

£250 for the illustration with the highest marks from the judging panel in the Children's Books section

Pentagram

The Pentagram Award

★ **award winners:** David Hughes *Little Robert* and *Eric Cantona*
Jason Ford *The Emerald Affair*
George Hardie *Umberto Verdi, Chimney Sweep*
Michael Sheehy *Demons of Desire, Godzilla Chicken* and *Escape from the Inferno*
Russell Walker *Mister Mondrian goes to the Seaside*

These artists have been selected by Pentagram to be promoted in an exhibition at their gallery in Notting Hill

DALER-ROWNEY
TRUSTED *by* ARTISTS WORLDWIDE

The Daler-Rowney Award

★ **award winner:** Roger Hulley *Beware of False Prophets who come in Sheep's Clothing*

£100-worth of art materials for the best use of traditional materials

DALER~ROWNEY
TRUSTED *by* ARTISTS WORLDWIDE

The Daler-Rowney Award for Outstanding Paper Sculpture

★ **award winner:** Gail Armstrong *Swimming Pool*

£50-worth of art paper for the best use of paper in illustration

WINSOR & NEWTON
The World's Finest Artists' Materials

The Windsor & Newton Award

★ **award winner:** Kevin Hauff *Rocket Man*

£100 for the best use of traditional materials

advertising

advertising

Dennis Willison / Senior Art Director / Saatchi & Saatchi

Annie Leonard / Art Buyer / Abbot Mead Vickers

Paddy Morahan / Project Manager / Bartle Bogle Hegarty

George Martin / Art Buyer / Ammarati Puris Lintas

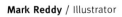

Mark Reddy / Illustrator

james marsh

21 Elms Road
London
SW4 9ER

t: 0171 622 9530
f: 0171 498 6851

★ **advertising section winner**
☆ *images 22* exhibitor

16
GB

title
La Bohème

medium
Acrylic on canvas

purpose of work
Posters and
brochures

brief
One in a set of six
paintings for
1997/98 Opera
Season

commissioned by
Heidi Bornstein

company
Seattle Opera

bill greenhead

1 Vicarage Crescent
London
SW11 3LP

t: 0171 228 8882

title
Tuff

medium
Pentel pens and
mechanical spot
colour

purpose of work
Comic cover for
Levi's

brief
Risqué comic cover
for the Levi's Mr
Boombastic
Campagin

commisioned by
Glenn

company
Tango/BBH

agent
Illustration
1 Vicarage Crescent
London
SW11 3LP
t: 0171 228 8882

andrew bylo

38B Southwell
Road
London
SE5 9PG

t: 0171 274 4116
f: 0171 738 3743

title
Wine Boxes

medium
Acrylic

purpose of work
Point of sale, beer
wine and spirits

brief
'Glyndebourne'-
style picnic using
bold rich warm
brushstrokes. Must
also be able to
take landscape
format section from
middle.

commissioned by
Paul Hutton

company
Safeway

MAGNET
ARTISTS

andrew bylo

38B Southwell
Road
London
SE5 9PG

t: 0171 274 4116
f: 0171 738 3743

title
Spain, Portugal and
Italy

medium
Acrylic

purpose of work
Point of sale for
beer, wines and
spirits

brief
Evoke mood and
feeling of country
of origin using bold
rich warm
brushstrokes. Must
be able to take
landscape format
section from
middle

commissioned by
Paul Hutton

company
Safeway

sue climpson

1 Vicarage Crescent
London
SW11 3LP

t: 0171 228 8882/8886

☆ *images 22* exhibitor

20
GB

title
Kenco Coffee - 1

medium
Photoshop, live
picture,
photography and
art work

purpose of work
Advertisement

brief
Kenco - given
outline requirement

commissioned by
Chris Mattey

company
Kenco Coffee

Agent
Illustration
1 Vicarage Crescent
London
SW11 3LP
t: 0171 228 8882

sue climpson

1 Vicarage Crescent
London
SW11 3LP

t: 0171 228 8882

title
Kenco Coffee - 2
medium
Photoshop, live
picture,
photography and
art work
purpose of work
Advertising

brief
Kenco - given
outline requirement
commissioned by
Chris Mattey
company
Kenco Coffee
agent
Illustration
1 Vicarage Crescent
London
SW11 3LP
t: 0171 228
8882/8886

adrian hardy

3 Vernon Road
Turnpike Lane
London N8 0QD

t: 0181 888 5275

title
La Tomatina

medium
Hand Montage

purpose of work
Advertising

brief
To advertise Gonzalez Byass Sherry. English man (Hugh Laurie type) abroad at the tomato throwing festival, Valencia

commissioned by
Gonzalez Byass

company
Simons Palmer

matilda harrison

c/- Arena
144 Royal College
Street
London
NW1 oTA

t: 0171 267 9661
f: 0171 284 0486

title
Dog

medium
Acrylic

purpose of work
Press advertising
campaign for
Purina Pro Plan

brief
To promote a
healthy dog who's
fed on Pro-Plan
dog food

commissioned by
Lindsey Winton

company
Saatchi & Saatchi

agent
Arena
144 Royal College
Street
London
NW1 oTA
t: 0171 267 9661

paul hess

1 Vicarage Crescent
London
SW11 3LP

t: 0171 228 8882

24
GB

title
The Wizard of Oz
medium
Watercolour
purpose of work
Poster to promote
a pantomime

brief
To illustrate a
poster for the
Wizard of Oz that
appeals equally to
adults and children
commissioned by
Denise Winford

company
Dundee Rep
Theatre

agent
Illustration
1 Vicarage Crescent
London
SW11 3LP
t: 0171 228 8882

clare mackie

21A Ursula Street
London
SW11 3DW

t: 0171 223 8649
f: 0171 223 8649

GB

title
Ostracised

medium
Watercolour

purpose
Harvey Nichols
store card,
application form
and newspaper ads

brief
To create an
amusing and
enticing image to
appeal to Harvey
Nichols shopping
types so that they
snap up their store
cards

commissioned by
Ruan
Milborrow/Mark
Nightingale

company
Harari Page

client
Harvey Nichols

agent
Eileen McMahon
and Co
PO Box 1062
Bayonne
New Jersey
07002
USA
t: 001 201 436 4362

clare mackie

21A Ursula Street
London
SW11 3DW

t: 0171 223 8649
f: 0171 223 8649

title
The Lover

medium
Watercolour and ink

purpose
"Happy-family-card style" travelator posters for underground stations

brief
To produce an illustration to work with the photographed gift Harvey Nichols were wanting business men to buy for their partner's Christmas gift

commissioned by
Ruan Milborrow/Mark Nightingale

company
Harari Page

client
Harvey Nichols

title
The Mother-in-Law

medium
Watercolour and ink

purpose
"Happy-family-card style" travelator posters for underground stations

brief
To produce an illustration to work with the photographed gift Harvey Nichols were wanting businessmen to buy for their mother-in-law's Christmas gift

commissioned by
Ruan Milborrow/Mark Nightingale

company
Harari Page

client
Harvey Nichols

21 Elms Road
London
SW4 9ER

t: 0171 622 9530
f: 0171 498 6851

title
Florencia in the
Amazon

medium
Acrylic on canvas

purpose of work
Posters and
brochures

brief
One in a set of six
paintings for
1997/98 Opera
Season

commissioned by
Heidi Bornstein

company
Seattle Opera

title
The Elixir of Love

medium
Acrylic on canvas

purpose of work
Posters and
brochures

brief
One in a set of six
paintings for
1997/98 Opera
Season

commissioned by
Heidi Bornstein

company
Seattle Opera

mark oliver

1 Vicarage Crescent
London
SW11 3LP

t: 0171 228 8882

☆ *images 22* exhibitor

title
Nuclear Plant
medium
Gouache
purpose of work
Advertisement

brief
Part of an ongoing
campaign designed
to demonstrate, in
a humourous way,
the need for
financial planning
commissioned by
Steve Rowlinson
company
Smarts Advertising
client
Templeton

title
Feet on the Seat
medium
Gouache
purpose of work
Poster/tube card for
South West trains

brief
To illustrate an
inconsiderate
character with
muddy feet on the
train seats
commissioned by
Chris Vane
company
The Workhouse
client
South West Trains

agent
Illustration
1 Vicarage Crescent
London
SW11 3LP
t: 0171 228 8882

sarah perkins

37E Guinness Crt
Snowfields
London
SE1 3SX

t: 0171 378 1510
f: 0171 357 6442

29

GB

title
Cheltenham
Literature Festival

medium
Mixed

purpose of work
Poster

brief
A colourful and
eyecatching poster
with the theme of
reading and writing

commissioned by
Sarah Smith

company
Cheltenham Town Hall

agent
The Inkshed
98 Columbia Road
London
E2 7QB
t: 0171 613 2323

georgia peters

112 Beulah Road
Thornton Heath
CR7 8JF

t: 0956 304 741

title
Queen Mother
'Garden'

medium
Inks

purpose of work
Invitation
card/painting

brief
To illustrate the
'garden' built for
the Queen Mother's
95th birthday

commissioned by
Christine Gray
Public Relations
and Promotion
Officer

company
English Heritage

agent
Thorogood
Illustration
5 Dryden Street
Covent Garden
London WC2E 9NW
t: 0171 829 8468

katie pratt

c/- Royal College of Art
Kensington Gore
London
SW3

title
Hakuhodo UK Ltd
purpose of work
Projector
advertising

brief
Computer press
advertising
commissioned by
Peter Cotton,
Abacus
agent
David Dalley
Hakuhodo UK
t: 0171 580 3900

c/- Folio
10 Gate Street
London
WC2A 3HP

t: 0171 242 9562

title
Animal

medium
Acrylic

purpose of work
Advertising

brief
Campaign to launch
computer games
video (pepperami)

commissioned by
George Martin

company
Ammirati
Puris/Lintas

agent
Folio
10 Gate Street
London
WC2A 3HP
t: 0171 242 9562

sorayama

c/- Bartle Bogle
Hegarty
60 Kingly Street
London
W1R 6DS

t: 0171 734 1677

33

GB

title
Before/After - Date

medium
Mixed

purpose of work
Advertising

brief
Advertising the 'Lynx'
range of male body
sprays, in a campaign
which appeals to the
14-24 male target
audience

commissioned by
Tiger Savage

company
Bartle Bogle Hegarty

agent
Miharu Yamutoto
Artspace Company
201 E 28th Street 15H
New York
10016
t:001 212 252 9122

simon spilsbury

CIA
36 Wellington Street
London WC2

t: 0171 240 8925

images 22 exhibitor

34
GB

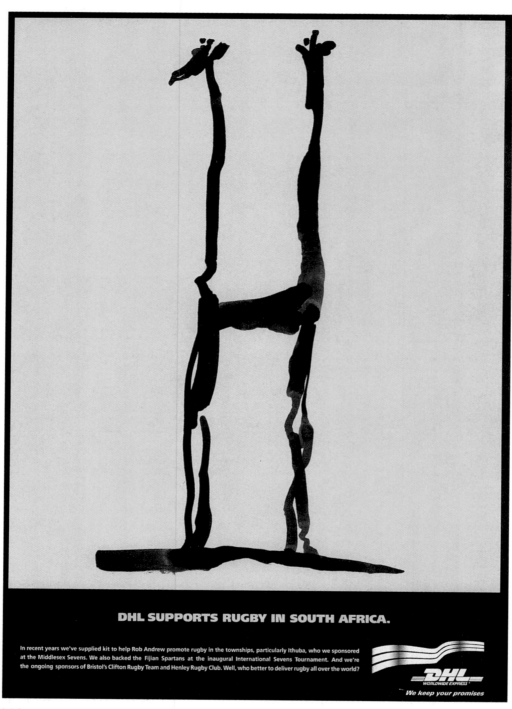

title
Giraffe Post

medium
Inks

purpose of work
Advertising

brief
To illustrate
giraffes as rugby
posts

commissioned by
Ken Sara

company
Mellors Reay

client
DHL

agent
CIA
36 Wellington
Street
London
WC2
t: 0171 240 8925

ADVERTISING

title
Rory Underlomu

medium
Ink

purpose of work
Advertising

brief
To illustrate growth
of *The Guardian's*
sports section

commissioned by
Dave Dye

company
Leagas Delaney

client
The Guardian

agent
CIA
36 Wellington
Street
London
WC2
t: 0171 240 8925

children's books

children's books
judges

Chris Inns / Deputy Art Director / Penguin Children's Books

Sarah Hodder / Art Director / Orchard Books

Judith Elliott / Director / Orion Children's Books

Stephen Cartwright / Illustrator

Mike Watts / Deputy Art Director, Fiction / Harper Collins Children's Books

andrew davidson

Moors Cottage
Swells Hill
Burleigh
Stroud
GL5 2SP

t: 01483 884 650
f: 01453 887 012

★ **children's books section winner**
★ **winner:** *The Transworld Children's Book Award*
☆ *images 22* exhibitor

title
Godhanger Series
medium
Wood engraving
purpose of work
Children's book
illustration

brief
Illustrate a passage
in Dick King-
Smith's book
Godhanger, a
symbolically
religious narrative
commissioned by
Ian Butterworth
company
Transworld
Publishing
agent
The Artworks
70 Rosaline Road
London SW16 7RT
t: 0171 610 1801

alex ayliffe

86 High Street
Codicote
Herts S94 8XE

t: 01438 821446

title
Oh No, Anna!
medium
Paper collage
purpose of work
to provide a
concept about
colours for pre-
school children

brief
To illustrate a
picture book with
flaps
commissioned by
Levinson Children's
Books

rowan barnes-murphy

Crossing cottage
North Charford
Fordingbridge
Hants
SP6 2DS

t: 01725 512 774
f: 01725 512 759

title
A Lick of the Spoon
medium
Pen, ink,
watercolour, crayon
purpose of work
To amuse

brief
To provide lively,
amusing
illustrations that
reflect the theme of
each poem to
appeal to children
of 6-8 years
commissioned by
Heather Richards
company
Cambridge
University Press
client
Cambridge Reading

title
A Lick of the Spoon
medium
Pen, ink,
watercolour, crayon
purpose of work
To amuse

brief
To provide lively,
amusing
illustrations that
reflect the theme of
each poem to
appeal to children
of 6-8 years
commissioned by
Heather Richards
company
Cambridge
University Press
client
Cambridge Reading

alison bartlett

22 Clovelly Road
St Georges
Bristol
BS5 7LS

t: 01179 540 966

title
Cat Among the
Cabbages
medium
Acrylic
purpose of work
Illustrations for
children's picture
book with flaps

brief
To illustrate a
picture book with
flaps about a cat's
journey through a
farmyard. The
book is for pre-
school children and
illustrates size and
colour concepts.
commissioned by
Levinson Children's
Books

tiphanie beeke

24 Northview Road
New Costessey
Norwich
Norfolk NR5 0BG

t: 01603 744588

title
The Brand New
Creature
medium
Watercolour and
acrylic
purpose of work
Illustrations for
children's picture
book

brief
To illustrate a
children's picture
book about
searching for a
crocodile and
capturing the heat,
colour and wildlife
of Africa
commissioned by
Tiffany Leeson

company
Levinson Children's
Books

derek brazell

28 Hatton House
Hindmarsh Close
London
E1 8JH

t: 0171 265 1896
f: 0171 265 1896

43

GB

title
Pig-Heart Boy
medium
Pencil and
Watercolour
purpose of work
Book cover

brief
To choose an
image from the
book that would
make an eye-
catching cover
commissioned by
Peter Bennett
company
Transworld
Publishers
agent
Artist Partners
14-18 Ham Yard
Great Windmill
Street
London W1V 8DE
t: 0171 734 7991
f: 0171 287 0371

frances cony

21 Tyndalls Park
Road
Bristol
BS8 1PQ

t: 0117 973 0022
f: 0117 973 0022

title
A Blushing Zebra!

medium
Pen and ink and
watercolour

purpose of work
Children's flap-
book illustration

brief
To answer the joke
'What's black and
white and red all
over?' - the
question being
printed on a
shower curtain flap
in *Zebra Jokes*
book

commissioned by
Sheri Safran

company
Sadie Fields
Productions Ltd

client
Tango Books

allan drummond

The White House
High Street
Dedham
CO7 6HL

t: 01206 322 360
f: 01206 322 360

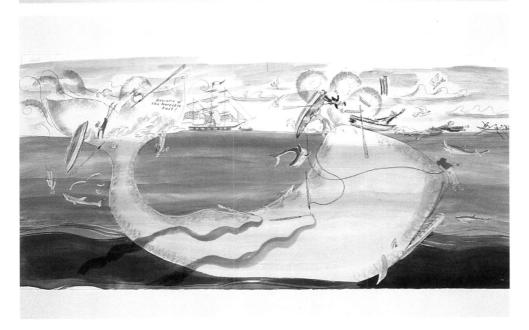

title
Moby Dick

medium
pen, watercolour

purpose
Cover and
illustrations for
children's book

brief
Illustrations to the
artist's own
adaptation of *Moby
Dick* for children,
written, designed
and illustrated by
the artist

commissioned by
Francesca Dow

company
Orchard Books

sara fanelli

Flat 11
Howitt Close
Howitt Road
London NW3 4LX

t: 0171 483 2544
f: 0171 483 2544

46

GB

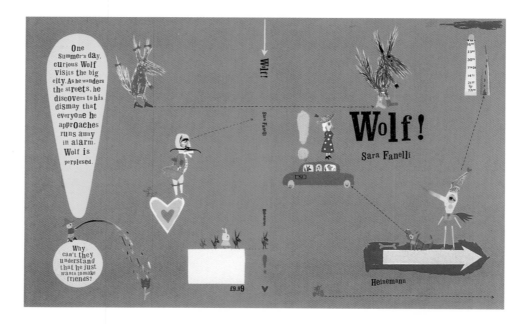

title
Wolf!

medium
Collage

purpose
Children's book

brief
Children's book

commissioned by
Heinemann

company
Reed Books

teresa flavin

Wellpark Enterprise
Centre
120 Sydney Street
Glasgow
G31 1JF

t: 0141 550 4994
f: 0141 550 4443

title
Tomkin Opens the
Rainclouds

medium
Acrylic on paper

purpose of work
Illustration for a
fairy tale

brief
Illustration for
*Tomkin and the
Three-Legged Stool*
by Vivian French
for the anthology
*Classic Fairy Tales
to Read Aloud*

commissioned by
Caroline Johnson

company
Kingfisher Books

agent
Publisher 's
Graphics (North
America only)
251 Greenwood Ave
Bethel, CT 06801
USA
t: (203) 797 8188

andy hammond

Benington House
93 Aylesbury Road
Wendover
HP22 6JN

t: 01296 624439
f: 01296 696198

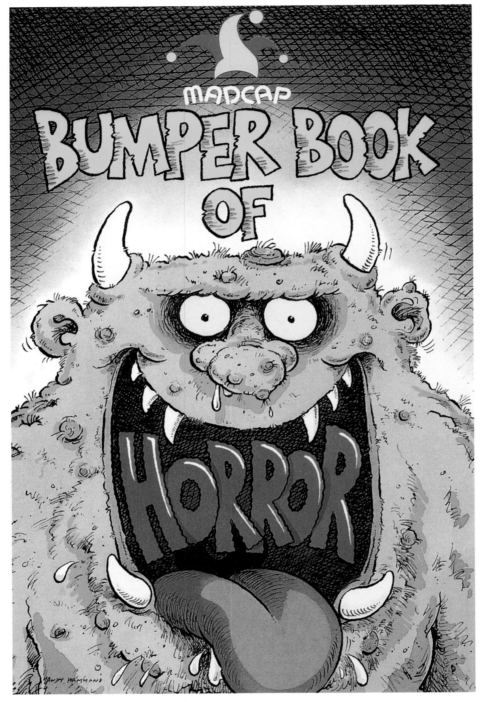

title
Bumper Book of
Horror

medium
Ink and
watercolour

purpose of work
Book cover

brief
To design a series
of book covers for
Andre Deutsch
'Madcap' 'Bumper
Book of...' -
children's jokes
and stories

commissioned by
Stephanie Goodwin

company
Andre Deutsch

agent
Illustration
1 Vicarage Crescent
London
SW11 3LP
t: 0171 228 8882

paul hess

1 Vicarage Crescent
London
SW11 3LP

t: 0171 228 8882
f: 0171 228 8886

49

GB

title
What's for Supper?
and Take the
Money and Run

medium
Watercolour

purpose of work
Book illustration

brief
Illustrate scenes
from *Jack and the
Beanstalk*

commissioned by
Joanna Devereux

company
Macdonald Young
Books

agent
Illustration
1 Vicarage Crescent
London
SW11 3LP
t: 0171 228 8882

david hughes

Rosemount Studios
43 Station Road
Marple Cheshire
SK6 6AJ

t: 0161 427 3852
f: 0161 427 8100

50

GB

title
Little Robert
medium
Pencil, watercolour, gouache
purpose
Book

brief
Story written and illustrated by the artist. A tale of Little Robert's Piano Lessons. Published in Germany
commissioned by
Abraham and Anne Teuter
company
Alibaba Verlag Nordendstrasse 20 6318 Frankfurt am Main Germany
t: 0049 6959 0097

stewart lees

Folio
10 Gate Street
Lincoln's Inn Fields
London W2 3HP

t: 0171 242 9562

51

GB

title
Anna Growing Up
on the Farm

medium
Oils

purpose of work
Book illustration

brief
To illustrate in a
realistic style a
series of poems for
children describing
incidents in the life
of a little girl living
on a farm

commissioned by
Jenny Bruce

company
Brimax Books

agent
Folio
10 Gate Street
Lincoln's Inn Fields
London
WC2 3HP
t: 0171 242 9562

keren ludlow

28 Hamilton Road
London
W5 2EH

t: 0181 567 2653
f: 0181 566 1462

52
GB

title
Café at the Edge of
the Moon
medium
Gouache
purpose of work
Children's book

brief
Children's book
commissioned by
Judith Elliott
company
Orion Children's
Books

james marsh

21 Elms Road
London
SW4 9ER

t: 0171 622 9530
f: 0171 498 6851

title
The Puffin Treasury
of Classics

medium
Acrylic on canvas

purpose of work
Book cover

brief
To convey the
various elements
contained in this
collection/panel for
type

commissioned by
Ronnie Fairweather/
Chris Inns

company
Penguin Books

client
Penguin Books

adrian reynolds

86 Chesterton Road
Cambridge
CB4 1ER

t: 01223 564 977

title
Harry and the
Snow King
medium
Watercolour and
pen
purpose of work
Illustrations for
children's book

brief
To illustrate a
winter's tale with
magical depths for
children from 3 to 7
commissioned by
Louise Millar
company
Levinson Children's
Books
agent
David Higham
Associates
5-8 Lower John
Street
Golden Square
London
W1R 4HA

piers sanford

33 Malden Hill
Gardens
New Malden
KT3 4HS

t: 0181 942 4135
f: 0181 942 4135

55

GB

title
Sam and Mr
Wallace

medium
Ink, colour wash

purpose of work
Book cover

brief
To depict a four-
year-old boy, Sam,
sitting in a tree
house with his toy
rabbit, 'Mr Wallace'

commissioned by
Kate Roberts

company
Walker Books

peter warner

Peter Warner's Studio
Hillside Road
Tatsfield
Kent
TN16 2NH
England

t: 01959 577270
f: 01959 541 414
m: 0958 531 538

title
Squirrels in the
School

medium
Watercolour

purpose of work
Cover design for
one of an ongoing
series of children's
paperbacks

brief
Emphasis is on
animal appeal.
The direct, loose,
spontaneous
approach was
devised for the
series, now very
successful.
Prepatory drawings
are kept minimal.

commissioned by
Claire Sutton

company
Hodder and
Stoughton

client
Hodder Children's
Books

bee willey

35 Fournier Street
London
E1 6QE

t: 0171 375 0323
f: 0171 375 0323

GB

title
The Arm Chair
Traveller

medium
Mixed

purpose of work
Part of a collection
of illustrations for a
book of myths and
legends: *The
Bronze Cauldron*

brief
Opening illustration
for a Hindu god
who travelled the
world by reading
and eating

commissioned by
Judith Elliott

company
Orion Children's
Books

agent
Caroline Walsh at
David Higham
Lower John Street
London W1
t: 0171 437 7888

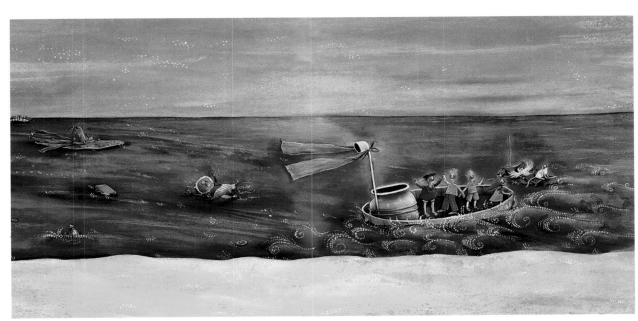

title
Nonsense Songs

medium
Mixed

purpose of work
Book Cover for
Nonsense Songs

brief
To make a cover
for a collection of
nonsense songs by
Edward Lear
depicting the main
characters ie 'The
Pobble', 'The
Jumblies', 'The Owl
and the Pussycat',
and 'The Quangle
Wangle's Hat'

commissioned by
Judith Elliott

company
Orion Children's
Books

agent
Caroline Walsh at
David Higham
5-8 Lower John
Street
London W1
t:0171 437 7888

editorial

Deborah George / Art Editor / *New Scientist* Magazine

Colin McHenry / Group Art Director / *Creative Review*

Anne Braybon / Art Director / *Rx* Magazine

Anne Morrow / Illustration Editor / *Weekend Guardian*

Peter Till / Illustrator

david hughes

Rosemount Studios
43 Station Road
Marple
SK6 6AJ

t: 0161 427 3852
f: 0161 427 8100

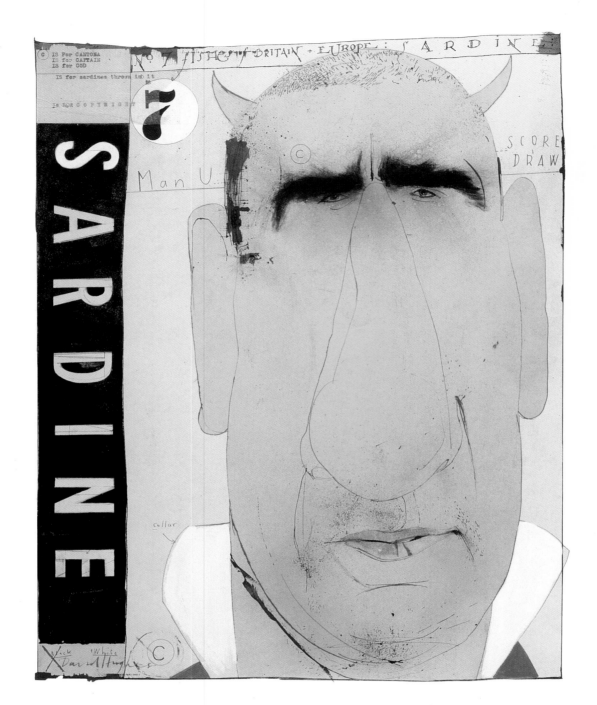

title
Eric Cantona

medium
Pen and ink,
watercolour,
charcoal and
gouache

purpose of work
Full-page
illustration for *The
Times* Magazine

brief
A portrait of Eric
Cantona

commissioned by
David Curless

client
The Times

paul blow

Flat 4
68 St Aubyns
Hove
BN3 2TE

t: 01273 779737
f: 01273 779 737

title
Passing Off

medium
Acrylic

purpose of work
Editorial

brief
Illustrate the problem of companies using well-known trade names to pass off their own products

commissioned by
Steve Aylett

commissioned by
New Law Journal

stuart briers

33 Eswyn Road
Tooting
London
SW17 8TR

t: 0181 767 2618
f: 0181 767 2618

62
GB

title
In Command

medium
Acrylic

purpose of work
Editorial illustration

brief
To depict how the
computer can tame
family finances

client
Mary Franz

company
Family Pc Magazine

MAGNET
ARTISTS

bill butcher

Sans Works
1 Sans Walk
London
EC1R oLT

t: 0171 336 6642
f: 0171 251 2642

63
GB

title
London Rats

medium
Acrylic

purpose of work
Cover illustration
for *ES* Magazine

brief
To illustrate article
on the London rat
infestation, in a
menacing way

commissioned by
Alison Pincott

company
ES Magazine

christopher gilvan-cartwright

36 Wellington Street
London WC2E 7BD

t: 0171 240 8925
f: 0171 836 1177

title
The Great Escape:
Commuter's Guide
to the Southwest

medium
Acrylic

purpose of work
Cover in a series of
six weekly
commuter guides

brief
Aspirational view
evoking the South-
West commuter
belt

commissioned by
Anne Braybon

company
Sunday Telegraph

agent
The Central
Illustration Agency
36 Wellington
Street London
WC2E 7BD
t: 0171 240 8925

jovan djordjevic

9 Fairlop Road
London
E11 1BL

t: 0181 539 3892
f: 0181 539 3893

title
Different for Girls

medium
Montage and ink

purpose of work
Editorial - money matters in *The Observer*

brief
Unlike gay men, lesbians who come out still face enormous hostilities at work

company
The Observer

emma dodd

Black Hat Studio
4 Northington
Street
Bloomsbury
London
WC1N 2JG

t: 0171 430 9163
f: 0171 430 9156

66
GB

title
Scientist and
Fingerprint
medium
Illustrator software
purpose of work
News story in
Gardener's World
Magazine
brief
Article about
counteracting the
trade in fake plants
by identifying
individual plant
cells, similar to
police use of DNA
fingerprinting

commissioned by
Abigail Dodd
company
BBC Gardener's
World
agent
Dave Morrison
Black Hat Studio
4 Northington Street
Bloomsbury
London WC1N 2JG
t: 0171 430 9146

max ellis

8 Elfin Lodge
Elfin Grove
Teddington
TW11 8RE

t: 0976 242 378
t/f: 0181 977 8924

67
GB

title
Every Body Hurts
medium
Digital sampling
montage
purpose of work
To accompany an
article

brief
illustrate a feature
on back injury in
the music biz
(specifically
guitarists)
commissioned by
Tony Horkins
company
IPC
client
Melody Maker

simon fell

87 Rothschild Road
London
W4 5NT

t: 0181 994 6206
f: 0181 994 6206

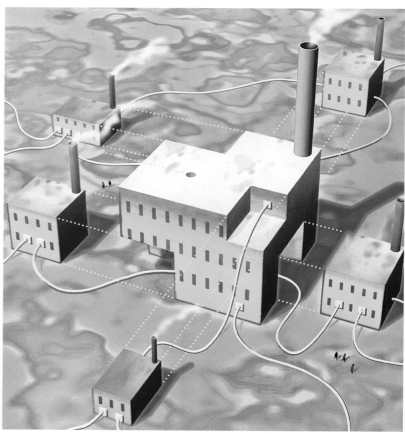

title
The Year 2000 and the Internet

medium
Colour copy and acrylic

purpose of work
Magazine illustration

brief
Problems caused by computer software that does not recognise the turn of the century could be transmitted across the internet

commissioned by
K Falconer

company
Network Reseller

client
Dennis Publishing

title
Contracting Out

medium
Computer generated (Bryce 2.0 and Photoshop 3.0)

purpose of work
Magazine article

brief
Companies are finding it is more efficient to contract out large parts of their administration, leaving them to concentrate on their core business

commissioned by
Gene Cornelius

company
The Engineer

client
Miller Freeman Technical

jason ford

c/- Heart
2nd Floor,
1 Tysoe Street
London
EC1R 4SA

t: 0171 833 4447

69
GB

title
The Emerald Affair

medium
Acrylic and ink

purpose of work
Illustration for
Radio 2 programme

brief
"I saw him as a
symptom of the
age...a man always
out to make a
profit."

commissioned by
Matthew Bookman

company
Radio Times

agent
Heart
2nd Floor
1 Tysoe Street
London
EC1R 4SA
t: 0171 833 4447

geoff grandfield

30 Allen Road
London
N16 8SA

t: 0171 241 1523

title
Rural Ride

medium
Pastel

purpose of work
Illustrate weekly
column on rural life

brief
Respond to
narrative on rural
burglary, Film Noir
mood

commissioned by
Anne Braybon

company
*The Sunday
Telegraph*

brian grimwood

36 Wellington St
London
WC2E 7BD

t: 0171 240 8925
f: 0171 836 1177

title
John Galliano
medium
Gouache
purpose of work
The Sunday Telegraph Magazine

brief
Saint or sinner section
commissioned by
Anne Braybon
company
The Sunday Telegraph Magazine
agent
CIA
36 Wellington Street
London
WC2E 7BD
t: 0171 240 8925
e.mail: c.illustration a@dail.pipex.com

brian grimwood

36 Wellington St
London
WC2E 7BD

t: 0171 240 8925
f: 0171 836 1177

title
The Last Word

medium
Gouache

purpose of work
Editorial

brief
Illustrate the article

commissioned by
John Belknap

company
The Express

agent
CIA
36 Wellington Street
London
WC2E 7BD
t: 0171 240 8925
e.mail:
c.illustrationa@dail.pipex.com

brian grimwood

36 Wellington St
London
WC2E 7BD

t: 0171 240 8925
f: 0171 836 1177

title
Words and Music

medium
Gouache

purpose of work
Editorial

brief
To enhance the front cover of *The Guardian Review*

commissioned by
Simon Esterson,
Roger Browning

company
The Guardian

agent
36 Wellington Street
London
WC2E 7BD
0171 240 8925
e.mail:
c.illustrationa@dail.pipex.com

george hardie

Drounces
White Chimney
Row
Westbourne
Emsworth
PO10 8RS

t: 01243 377 528
f: 01243 370 769

74
GB

title
Umberto Verdi,
Chimney Sweep

medium
Ink and Xerox on
to coloured papers

purpose of work
Illustration for
Radio 4 play

brief
A bored and lonely
mum chooses the
most romantic
name when her
chimney needs
cleaning. Will
Umberto's Latin
touch sweep her
off her feet?

commissioned by
Nathan Gale

company
Radio Times

matilda harrison

c/- Arena
144 Royal College
Street
London
NW1 0TA

t: 0171 267 9661
f: 0171 284 0486

title
Castles in the Sand

medium
Acrylic

purpose of work
Full-page editorial
illustration for *The
Independent*
Magazine

brief
Fading love turns a
long-married
couple into
strangers on the
shore: extract from
a novel by Amy
Bloom

commissioned by
Gary Cochrane

company
The Independent

agent
Arena
144 Royal College
Street
London
NW1 0TH
t: 0171 267 9661

robert heesom

Wyatts
Rectory Drive
Bidborough
Tunbridge Wells
TN3 0UL

t: 01892 549084
f: 01892 549084

title
Networking
medium
Acrylic on canvas
purpose of work
To illustrate an
article in *PC
Magazine*

brief
How information
can be passed
around computer
networks. The
extra 'flying' hands
denote unseen
eavesdroppers
grabbing the
information
commissioned by
Hazel Bennington
company
Ziff-Davis UK
Limited
client
PC Magazine

title
Pass the Parcel
medium
Acrylic on canvas
purpose of work
To illustrate an
article in *PC
Magazine*

brief
ISDN 'routers' are
used to send
computer
information to the
right destination.
Here a postman re-
routes the packets
of information
commissioned by
Hazel Bennington
company
Ziff-Davis UK Ltd
client
PC Magazine

angela j hogg

56 Astbury Road
London
SE15 2NJ

t: 0171 732 5957

title
100th anniversary
of the electron

medium
Acrylic and collage

purpose of work
To illustrate a
magazine article

brief
To illustrate an
article about the
history past and
present of the
electron particle

commissioned by
New Scientist

agent
The Inkshed
98 Columbia Road
London
E2 7QB
t: 0171 613 2323

david hughes

Rosemount Studios
43 Station Road
Marple
Cheshire
SK6 6AJ

t: 0161 427 3852
f: 0161 427 8100

★ **award winner:** *The Pentagram Award*
☆ *images 22* exhibitor

title
Spanish Civil War
Film Festival

medium
Pen and ink,
watercolour and
gouache

purpose of work
To illustrate *What's
On* listings in New
York

brief
Gotta great job for
you, not the usual
portrait, can you
do us a piece
about the Spanish
Civil War?

commissioned by
Owen Phillips

client
The New Yorker
20 West 43 street
New York
NY 10036
USA

david hughes

Rosemount Studios
43 Station Road
Marple
Cheshire
SK6 6AJ

t: 0161 427 3852
f: 0161 427 8100

GB

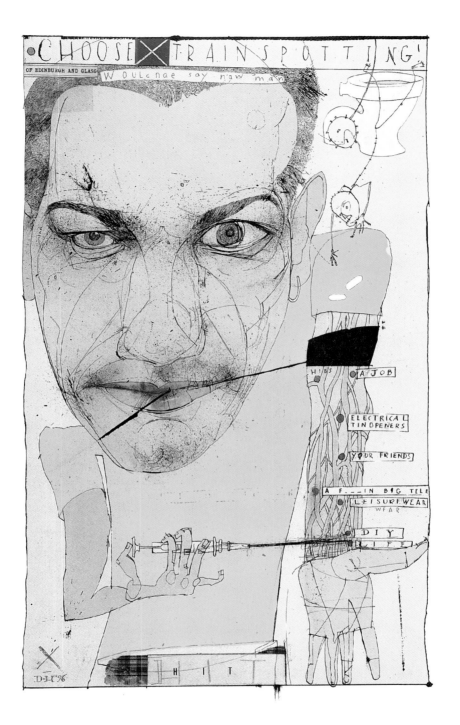

title
Trainspotting
medium
Ink and pen and
watercolour and
paper
purpose of work
Illustration for
video review for
Premiere Magazine

brief
Illustrate a video '
review for the film
'Trainspotting'
commissioned by
Sharon Cowen
client
Premiere Magazine
1633 Broadway
New York
NY 10019
USA

ciaran hughes

33 Reservoir Road
London
SE4 2NU

t: 0171 771 0615
f: 0171 771 0615
e.mail: thebhoys@dircon.co.uk

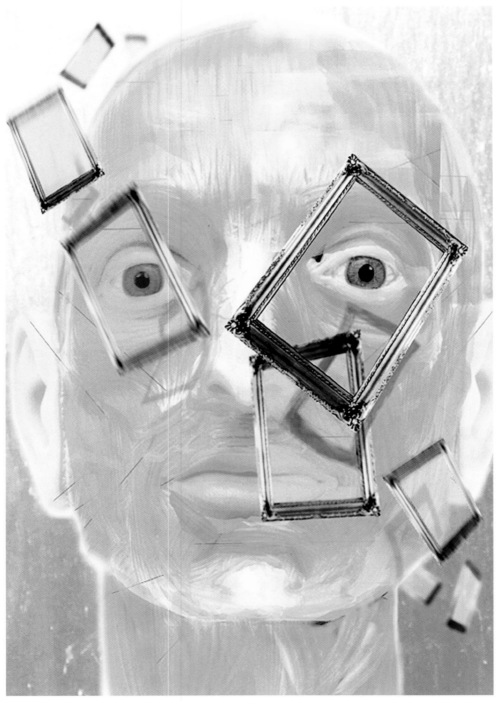

title
The Eye of the
Beholder

medium
Adobe Photoshop

purpose of work
Accompany article
on judging
competitions in a
magazine

brief
Show what it's like
to judge and be
judged in
competitions

commissioned by
Brendan Foley

company
Foley Associates

client
Communicators in
Business

satoshi kambayashi

Flat 2
40 Tisbury Road
Hove
East Sussex
BN3 3BA
t: 01273 771539
f: 01273 771539
pager: 01426 131519

title
The Nowhere Man
in Transit Lounge

medium
India ink and
watercolour

purpose of work
Editorial illustration
for *Prospect*
Magazine

brief
To illustrate an
essay by Pico Iyer
about the new
transcontinental
people for whom
home is everywhere
and nowhere

commissioned by
Susan Buchanan

company
Buchanan-Davey

client
Prospect Magazine

agent
Ian Fleming and
Associates
72-74 Brewer
Street, London
W1R 3PH
t: 0171 734 8701

satoshi kambayashi

Flat 2
40 Tisbury Road
Hove
East Sussex
BN3 3BA
t: 01273 771539
f: 01273 771539
pager: 01426 131519

82
GB

title
Treasure Trove
medium
India ink and
watercolour
purpose of work
Cover illustration
for *New Law
Journal*

brief
To produce a cover
illustration featuring
the article reviewing
the new Treasure Act
of 1996
commissioned by
Stephen Aylett
company
Butterworth & Co
Ltd
client
New Law Journal
agent
Ian Fleming and
Associates
72-74 Brewer Street
London
W1R 3PH
t: 0171 734 8701

satoshi kambayashi

Flat 2
40 Tisbury Road
Hove
East Sussex
BN3 3BA
t: 01273 771539
f: 01273 771539
pager: 01426 131519

title
Little Chef belongs
to the Granada
Group, too!

medium
India ink and
watercolour

purpose of work
Editorial illustration
for a food column

brief
To produce an
illustration for a
food column about
the two extremes
of the Granada
Empire - Savoy
River Room and
the Little Chef

commissioned by
Tom Reynolds

company
The Express
Newspapers plc

client
The Sunday
Express Magazine

agent
Ian Fleming and
Associates
t: 0171 734 8701

title
The Career Lies

medium
India ink and
watercolour

purpose of work
Editorial for Elle
German edition

brief
Illustrate career lies
for women. This
one is about the
common belief that
having a baby ruins
a woman's career

commissioned by
Karin Ecker-Spaniol

company
Burda/Elle Verlag

client
Elle German Edition

agent
Ian Fleming and
Associates
t: 0171 734 8701

gary kaye

Clockwork Studios
38b Southwell Road
London
SE5 9PG

t: 0171 274 1958
f: 0171 738 3743

title
Sixty Somethings
medium
Collage, gouache, and coloured pencils
purpose of work
Editorial

brief
To illustrate an article on the youthfulness and the spending power of the 60+ age group in today's society
commissioned by
Alison Hughes
company
East Central Studios
client
Viewpoint Magazine, Amsterdam

title
Portobello
medium
Collage, gouache, and coloured pencils
purpose of work
Editorial

brief
To illustrate the feel of Portobello Road

paul leith

37 Therapia Road
London
SE22 0SF

t: 0181 693 8886
f: 0181 693 8886

title
Hong Kong
medium
Acrylic and paper
purpose of work
Book review cover

brief
Illustrate book review for *The Economist* Magazine
commissioned by
The Economist
agent
Jacqui Figgis
Unit 4
Eel Brook Studios
125 Moore Park
Road
London
SW6 4PS
t: 0171 610 9933

397
Whalebone Lane
North Chadwell
Heath, Romford
RM6 6RH

t: 0181 597 2457
f: 0181 597 2457

86
GB

title
Helping Hand
medium
Acrylic
purpose of work
Editorial

brief
Illustrate article
recognizing nurses'
contribution in
building towards
client-centred care
in high security
hospitals

commissioned by
Nursing Times
Magazine

james marsh

21 Elms Road
London
SW4 9ER

t: 0171 622 9530
f: 0171 498 6851

title
Ice Age Politics

medium
Acrylic on canvas

purpose of work
Magazine feature

brief
Ecology feature
discussing the
environment and
endangered species

commissioned by
Susan Buchanan

company
Prospect magazine

shane mc gowan

Studio 204
Cable Street Studios,
Thames House
566 Cable Street
London
E1 9HB

t: 0171 791 2916
f: 0171 791 2916

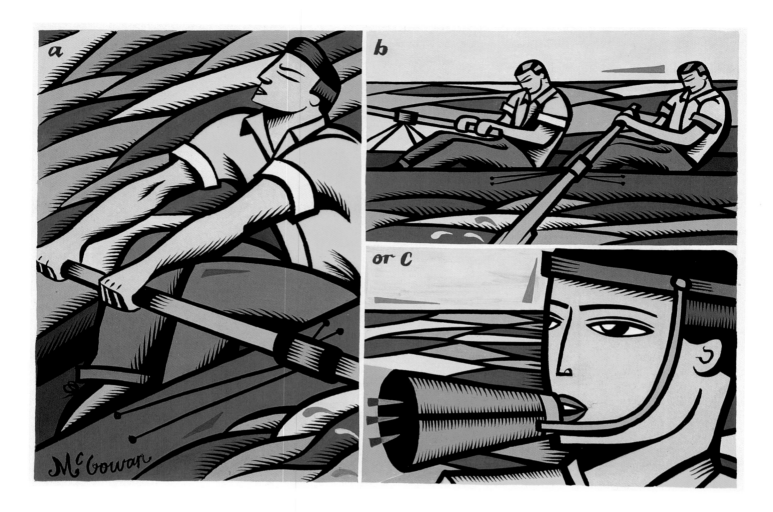

title
Tinker, Tailor, Sole
Trader, Partner...
medium
Gouache
purpose of work
To illustrate article
in business section

brief
To show that in
setting up a
business, you can
be sole trader, a
partner or a
company
commissioned by
Andy Bevan
company
The Observer
agent
The Organisation
69 Caledonian
Road
London
N1 9BT
t: 0171 833 8268

shane mc gowan

Studio 204
Cable Street Studios,
Thames House
566 Cable Street
London
E1 9HB

t: 0171 791 2916
f: 0171 791 2916

title
Be a Rock and
Listen
medium
Gouache
purpose of work
To illustrate article
in the health
section

brief
To show how
friends' sympathy
can be burdensome
when a partner is
seriously ill
commissioned by
Kevin Bayliss
company
The Independent
agent
The Organisation
69 Caledonian
Road
London
N1 9BT
t: 0171 833 8268

ingram pinn

33 Alexandra Road
Chiswick
London
W4 1AX

t: 0181 994 5311
f: 0181 747 8200

title
City Bonuses
medium
Pen and ink

brief
To illustrate an article about huge bonuses given to city dealers
commissioned by
Brana Radovic
company
The Financial Times

daniel pudles

8 Herschell Road
London
SE23 1EG

t: 0181 699 8540
f: 0181 699 8540

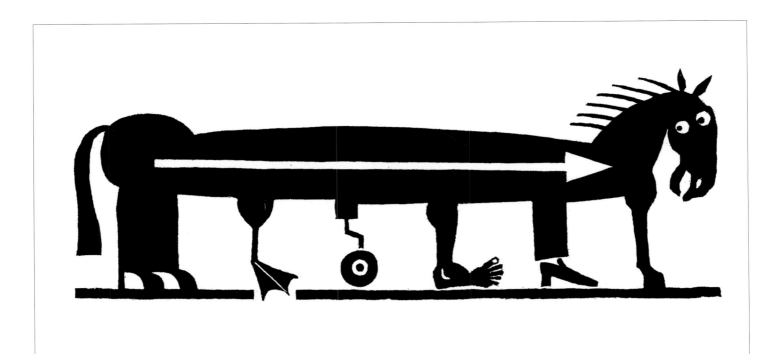

title	**brief**
The Grandeur that was Life	An article about evolution
medium	**company**
Print from woodcut	*The Guardian*
purpose of work	**client**
Illustration for *The Guardian*	Roger Browning

nik ramage

99a Newington Green Road
London N1 4QY

t: 0976 314 302

title
Italian Pot-Host

medium
3-D mixed media

purpose of work
To accompany food
article

brief
To depict the
generic host of
Italian restaurants

commissioned by
Linda Boyle

company
You Magazine, *Mail
on Sunday*

michael sheehy

115 Crystal Palace
Road
East Dulwich
London
SE22 9ES

t: 0181 693 4315
f: 0181 693 4315

93

GB

title
Escape from the
Inferno
medium
Mixed media
purpose of work
Newspaper
supplement cover

brief
The hazards of a fire
at work and how to
deal with it
commissioned by
Roger Browning
company
The Guardian
agent
CIA
36 Wellington Street
London
WC2E 7BD
t: 0171 240 8925

title
Demons of Desire
medium
Mixed media
purpose of work
Newspaper
supplement cover

brief
The obsessions of a
lover who cannot 'let
go' of a deceased
partner
commissioned by
Simon Esterson
company
The Guardian
agent
CIA
36 Wellington Street
London
WC2E 7BD
t: 0171 240 8925

david smith

65 Breech Lane
Walton on the Hill
Surrey KT20 7SJ

t: 01737 814 189
f: 01737 814 190

title
William Morris

medium
Collage

purpose of work
Cover illustration
for *The Sunday
Times* Culture
section

brief
Open brief to show
portrait of William
Morris

commissioned by
Julia Durman

company
News International

client
The Sunday Times

agent
East Wing
98 Columbia Road
London
E2 7QB
t: 0171 613 2323

blaise thompson

Big Orange
2nd Floor
Back Building
150 Curtain Road
London
EC2 3AR

t: 0171 739 765
f: 0171 613 2341

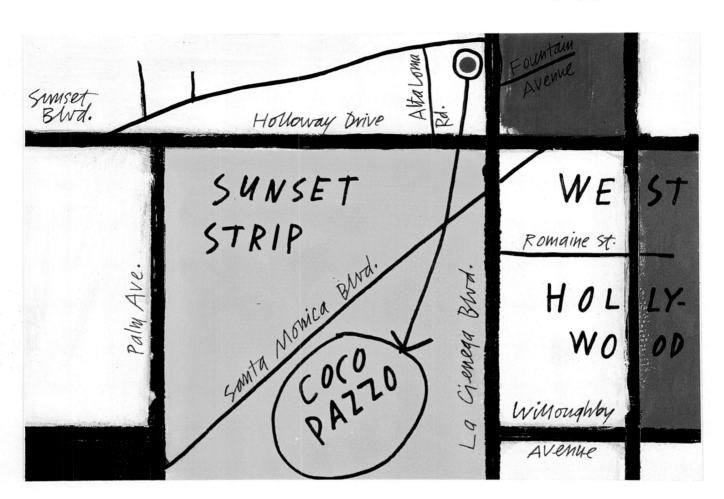

title
Restaurants (The
Mondrian Hotel)
medium
Acrylic

purpose of work
To illustrate
restaurant column

brief
To provide an
illustrated map
echoing mood of
article and locating
restaurant
commissioned by
Anne Braybon

company
*The Sunday
Telegraph*

alastair taylor

24 Watling Street
Thaxted
CM6 2PJ

t: 01371 831126
f: 01371 831321

title
An Aversion to
Herrings
medium
Acrylic
purpose of work
Magazine article on
'Food Notebook'
page

brief
The writer had a
deep revulsion for
herrings instilled in
him at school by
Miss Platt -
Assistant Matron
commissioned by
Wayne Ford
company
The Observer
agent
The Inkshed
98 Columbia Road
London
E2 7QB
t: 0171 613 2323

alastair taylor

24 Watling Street
Thaxted
CM6 2PJ

t: 01371 831126
f: 01371 831321

97

GB

title
Aga Louts
medium
Acrylic
purpose of work
Magazine article -
'Food Notebook'
page

brief
A backlash against
Agas and their
owners
commissioned by
Wayne Ford
company
The Observer
agent
The Inkshed
98 Columbia Road
London
E2 7QB
t: 0171 613 2323

chris winn

40 Taverham Road
Drayton
Norwich
NR8 6RY

t: 01603 860532
f: 01603 260112
e-mail: chris.winn@paston.co.uk

title
10 Downing Street

medium
Computer image

purpose of work
Illustrations for article in *The Sunday Telegraph*

brief
To illustrate the idea that fhe finely tuned machinery of Whitehall will barely miss a beat on the changeover in Government

commissioned by
Graeme Murdoch

company
The Sunday Telegraph

janet woolley

Janet Woolley
c/- Arena
144 Royal College
Street
London
NW1 0TA

t: 0171 267 9661
f: 0171 284 0486

title
Psychic Psmith on
Ice

medium
Mixed media

purpose of work
Mock horoscope
illustration

brief
To capture the
character 'Psychic
Psmith' in winter

commissioned by
Anne Braybon

company
*The Sunday
Telegraph*

agent
Arena
144 Royal College
Street
London
NW1 0TA
t: 0171 267 9661

general books

general books

Alison Barclay / Art Editor / Conran Octopus

Claire Ward / Art Director / Transworld Publishers

Fiona Carpenter / Art Director / Pan Macmillan

Paul Cox / Illustrator

Nick Austin / Senior Editor of Fiction / Hodder Stoughton

geoff grandfield

30 Allen Road
London
N16 8SA

t: 0171 241 1523
f: 0171 241 1523

102
GB

title
Stamboul Train

medium
Chalk pastel

purpose of work
From a series of
eight, to illustrate
the novel

brief
Scene from Graham
Greene's *Stamboul
Train*

commissioned by
Joe Whitlock-
Blundell

company
The Folio Society

nancy anderson

8A Birdhurst Rise
South Croydon
CR2 7ED

t: 0181 681 0310

title
Exploring Japan
medium
Linocut and
Watercolour
purpose of work
Book Cover

brief
The book is
concerned with
Japan's natural
hazards, transport,
fishing and
farming, industry,
pollution and
weather

MAGNET
ARTISTS

gail armstrong

1 Vicarage Crescent
London
SW11 3LP

t: 0171 228 8882

★ **award winner:** *The Daler Rowney Award for Outstanding Paper Sculpture*

title
Clown Heads

medium
Paper sculpture

purpose
Chapter heading
illustration

brief
To show how
people put a brave
face on when
depressed

commissioned by
Luke Herriot,
Sarah Mulligan

company
DK Direct

client
Mindpower

agent
Illustration
1 Vicarage Crescent
London SW11 3LP
t: 0171 228 8882

title
Swimming Pool

medium
Paper sculpture

purpose
To illustrate text

brief
To show different
personality types in
the pool of life

commissioned by
Luke Herriot,
Sarah Mulligan

company
DK Direct

client
Mindpower

graham austin

1 Vicarage Crescent
London
SW11 3LP

t: 0171 228 888

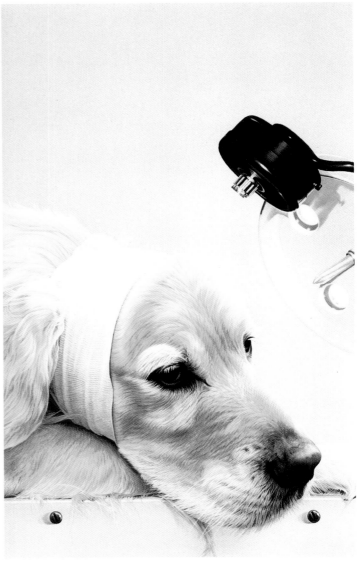

title
Torn Ear
medium
Watercolour and
body colour
purpose
Children's book
cover

brief
To illustrate a fox
cub that was
attacked by parents
commissioned by
Claire Sutton
client
Hodder Children's
Books
agent
Illustration
1 Vicarage Crescent
London SW11 3LP
t: 0171 228 8882

title
A Matter of Life
and Death
medium
Watercolour and
body colour
purpose
Children's book
cover

brief
To illustrate a
Golden Retriever in
pain at a vet's
table
commissioned by
Padd Cookson
client
Hodder Children's
Books
agent
Illustration
1 Vicarage Crescent
London SW11 3LP
t: 0171 228 8882

david bird

3 Natal Road
London
SW16 63A

t: 0181 769 5011

title
Letter back to
Ancient China

medium
CLC

purpose of work
Book cover

brief
Book cover design

commissioned by
Eric Lane

company
Dedalus

michael bramman

104 Dudley Court
Upper Berkeley St
London
W1H 7PJ

t: 0171 723 3564
f: 0171 723 3564

title
A Regular Guy

medium
Acrylic

purpose of work
Book cover

brief
Read manuscript
and produce an
illustration that
reflects and is
sympathetic to the
story

commissioned by
Kristina Langheim

company
Pentagram Design
Ltd

client
Faber & Faber

title
Bright Angel Time

purpose
Book Cover

medium
Acrylic

brief
Read manuscript
and produce an
illustration that
reflects and is
sympathetic to the
story

commissioned by
Kristina Langheim

company
Pentagram Design
Ltd

client
Faber & Faber

paul burgess

73 Pascoe Road
London
SE13 5JE

t: 0181 852 1600
f: 0181 852 1600

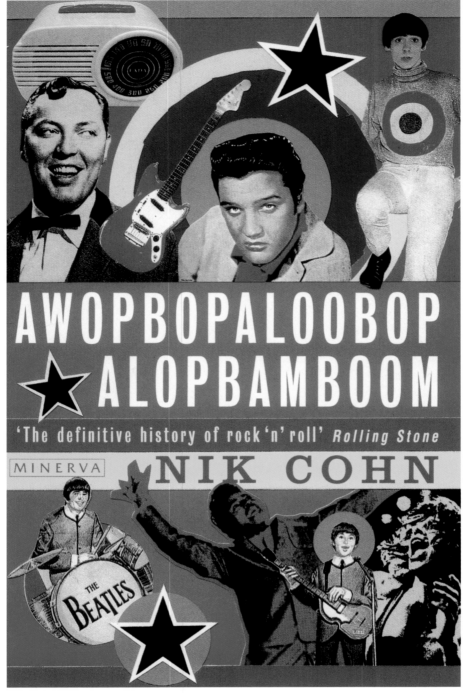

title
Awopbopaloobop
alopbamboom

medium
Collage

purpose of work
Paperback book
cover

brief
To produce a 'pop-
art'-based image
showing the range
of musical artists
featured in Nik
Cohn's writing

commissioned by
Jonathan Gray

company
Button Design/Reed
Books

agent
Private View
26 Levendale Road
London
SE23 2TW
t: 0181 291 1110

sara fanelli

Flat 11
Howitt Close
Howitt Road
London NW3 4LX

t: 0171 483 2544
f: 0171 483 2544

title
Family Terrorists by
A Nelson

medium
Collage

purpose of work
Book cover

brief
Book cover

commissioned by
Fiona Carpenter

company
Picador

geoff grandfield

30 Allen Road
London
N16 8SA

t: 0171 241 1523
f: 0171 241 1523

110
GB

title
The Confidential
Agent No 2

medium
Chalk pastel

purpose of work
From a series of
eight, to illustrate
the novel

brief
Scene from Graham
Greene's *The
Confidential Agent*

commissioned by
Joe Whitlock-
Blundell

company
The Folio Society

geoff grandfield

30 Allen Road
London
N16 8SA

t: 0171 241 1523
f: 0171 241 1523

title
A Gun for Sale

medium
Chalk pastel

purpose of work
From a series of
eight, to illustrate
the novel

brief
Scene from Graham
Greene's *A Gun For
Sale*

commissioned by
Joe Whitlock-
Blundell

company
The Folio Society

geoff grandfield

30 Allen Road
London
N16 8SA

t: 0171 241 1523
f: 0171 241 1523

☆ *images 22* exhibitor

title
The Confidential
Agent No 1

medium
Chalk pastel

purpose of work
From a series of
eight, to illustrate
the novel

brief
Scene from Graham
Greene's *The
Confidential Agent*

commissioned by
Joe Whitlock-
Blundell

company
The Folio Society

peter gudynas

89 Hazelwell Cresc
Stirchley
Birmingham
B30 2QE

t: 0121 459 0080
f: 0121 459 0080

title
Polymorph

medium
Photoshop

purpose of work
Book cover

brief
A novel about a 'polymorph' - a 'post human' being capable of changing its physical identity, anatomical structure, gender and race, set in near-future New York

commissioned by
Rich Hasselberger

client
Penguin Books USA

sara hayward

31 Diglis Road
Worcester
WR5 3BW

t: 01905 357 563
f: 01905 357 563

114

GB

title
Fruit

medium
Acrylic

purpose of work
Book illustration

brief
A lively and
energetic treatment
of fruit

commissioned by
Hazel Harrison

company
Quarto Publishing

malin lindgren

c/o The Inkshed
98 Columbia Road
London
E2 7QB

t: 0171 613 2323
f: 0171 613 2726

115
GB

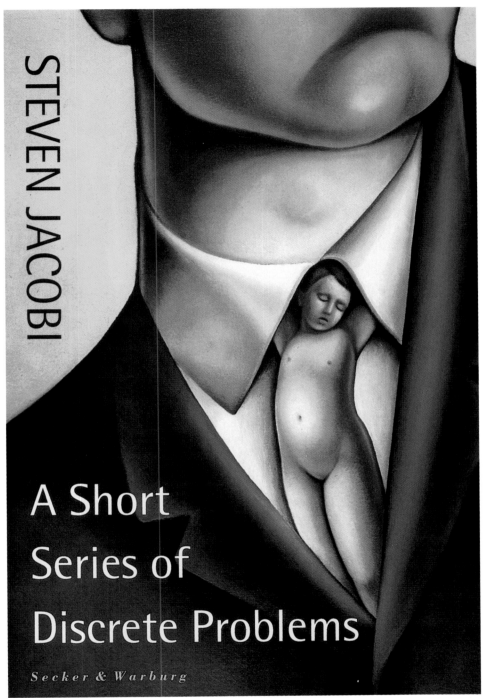

title
A Short Series of
Discrete Problems

medium
Alkyd Oils

purpose of work
Book cover for a
novel by Steven
Jacobi

brief
A novel about a
disturbed young
man who was born
female, and
following sexual
abuse from her
father, had a sex
change at 14

commissioned by
John Hamilton

company
Reed Consumer
Books

client
Secker & Warburg

agent
The Inkshed
98 Columbia Road
London E2 7QB
t: 0171 613 2323
f: 0171 613 2726

brigitte mcdonald

40 Knightlow Road
Harborne
Birmingham
B17 8QB

t: 0121 429 8655
f: 0121 429 8655

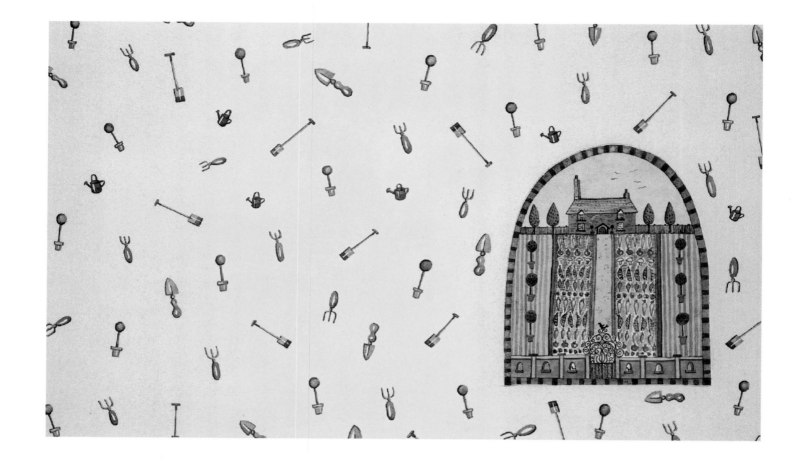

title
The Gardener
medium
Watercolour
purpose of work
Book cover and
interior illustration

brief
To illustrate a
cover for a
gardener's
notebook
commissioned by
Ljiljana Baird
company
Museum Quilts
Publications Ltd

sarah perkins

37E Guinness Crt
Snowfields
London
SE1 3SX

t: 0171 378 1510
f: 0171 357 6442

117

GB

title
Dr Neruda
medium
Mixed
purpose of work
Book cover

brief
Open brief based
on the book
commissioned by
Clare Ward
company
Transworld
Publishers
agent
The Inkshed
98 Columbia Road
London
E2 7QB
t: 0171 613 2323

paul powis

31 Diglis Road
Worcester
WR5 3BW

t: 01905 357 563
f: 01905 357 563

118

GB

☆ *images 22* exhibitor

title
Two Trees

medium
Acrylic

purpose of work
Book illustration

brief
Painting using bold
shapes and strong
colour

commissioned by
Hazel Harrison

company
Quarto Publishing

paul powis

31 Diglis Road
Worcester
WR5 3BW

t: 01905 357 563
f: 01905 357 563

119

GB

title
Polish chess
players in
Kensington
Gardens

medium
Acrylic

purpose of work
book illustration

brief
Paint figures in a
landscape, in a
simplified way

commissioned by
Hazel Harrison

company
Quarto Publishing

daniel pudles

8 Herschell Road
London
SE23 1EG

t: 0181 699 8540
f: 0181 699 8540

title
Vital Lies, Simple
Truths
medium
Print from woodcut
purpose of work
Cover illustration

brief
An analysis on the
ways we deceive
ourselves
company
Bloomsbury
client
William Webb

matthew richardson

Garden Cottage
Penpont
Brecon, Powys
LD3 8EU

t: 01874 636 269
f: 01874 636 269

title
How Babies
Become Conscious
(The Secret
Language of the
Mind)

medium
Mixed media

purpose of work
Book chapter
illustration

brief
When babies are
born they are not
conscious of
themselves as
separate entities.
As they develop,
they learn the
boundaries between
themselves and
other people and
objects

commissioned by
Paul Reid

company
Mitchell Beazley
DBP

company
Duncan Baird
Publishers

agent
Jacqui Figgis
Unit 4
Eel Brook Studios
125 Moore Park
Road London
SW6 4PS
t: 0171 610 9933

david smith

65 Breech Lane
Walton-on-the-Hill
Surrey KT20 7SJ

t: 01737 814 189
f: 01737 814 190

122
GB

title
Orlando Crisp's
Flesheater
Cookbook

medium
Montage

purpose of work
Book cover
commission

brief
Book cover design

commissioned by
D Bird, E Lane

company
Dedalus

agent
East Wing
98 Columbia Road
London E2 7QB
t: 0171 613 5580

sharif tarabay

1 Vicarage Crescent
London
SW11 3LP

t: 0171 228 8882

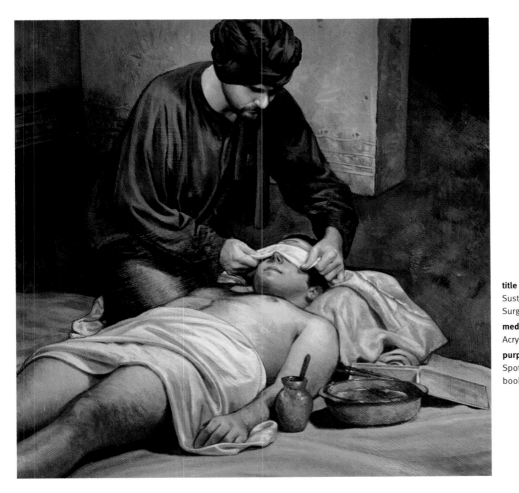

title
Sustuta - Nose
Surgery

medium
Acrylic

purpose of work
Spot illustration for
book

brief
Spot illustration to
show early
medicine for
history news series,
for Walker Books

agent
Illustration
1 Vicarage Crescent
London
Sw11 3LP
t: 0171 288 8882

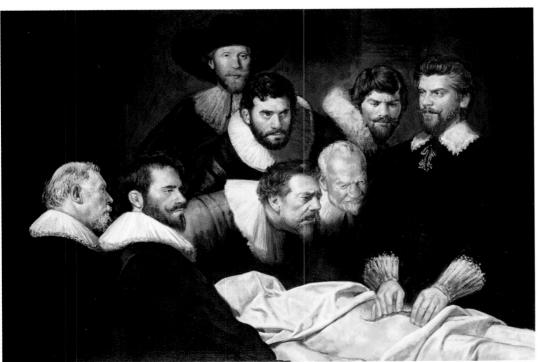

title
Versalius -
Anatomy Lesson

medium
Acrylic

purpose of work
Spot illustration for
book

brief
Spot illustration to
show early
medicine for
history news series,
for Walker Books

agent
Illustration
1 Vicarage Crescent
London
SW11 3LP
t: 0171 228 8882

sue williams

c/o Folio
10 Gate Street
Lincoln's Inn Fields
London WC 2A 3HP

t: 0171 242 9562

title
The Persian Pickle
Club
medium
Pastel, coloured
crayon
purpose of work
Book cover for
novel by Sandra
Dallas

brief
Illustrate novel set
in hot, dry, rural
landscape of Kansas
in the 1930s. Plot
holds together
around a group of
women meeting to
make a quilt so the
decorative pattern
of illustration
echoes this as well
as depicting some
characters in the
plot
commissioned by
Sally Munford
company
Random House
Publishing
agent
Folio
10 Gate Street
Lincoln's Inn Fields
London WC2A 3HP
t: 0171 242 9562

title
That Bad Woman
medium
Pastel, coloured
crayon
purpose of work
Book cover of That
Bad Woman, a
collection of short
stories by Clare
Boylan

brief
Image to represent
stories focusing on
contemporary
women and issues
of responsibility
and choice/
ordinary women
showing their
potential when
thwarted
commissioned by
Peter Cotton
company
Little, Brown
agent
Folio
10 Gate Street
Lincoln's Inn Fields
London
WC2E 3HP
t: 0171 242 9562

9 Sussex Road
Colchester
CO3 3QH

t: 01206 577766

125
GB

title
Mr Mondrian goes
to the Seaside

medium
Ink

purpose of work
Contribution to
University of
Brighton Book

brief
Produce an image
for a book on the
theme of 'Summer'

commissioned by
MA Books

client
MA Books

information & technical

Tony Blurton / Director / Four IV

Janette Earney / Freelance Art Director

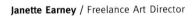

Jayne Jones / Project Art Director / Dorling Kindersley

Don Jessop / Architectural Illustrator

Anthony Johnson / Senior Designer / Michael Peters Ltd

tilly northedge

10 Barley Mow
Passage
London
W4 4PH

t: 0181 994 6477
f: 0181 995 3049

128
GB

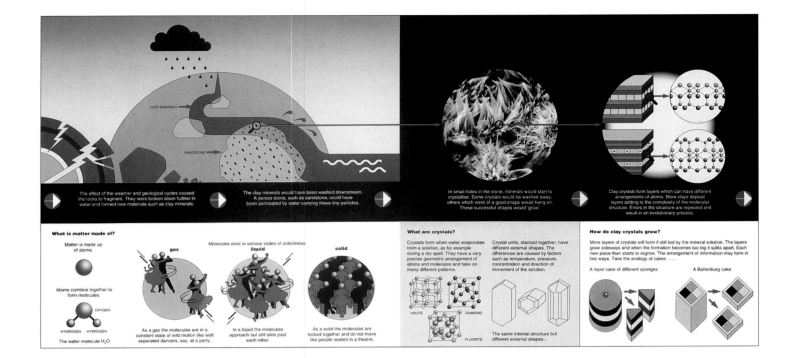

title
How Did Life
Begin? - 2

medium
Computer artwork

purpose of work
Self promotion

brief
A self-set brief to
research and
explain a theory of
how life began and
also to learn
computer skills

geoffrey appleton

New York Farm
Upper Elkstone
Onecote Leek
Staffs
ST13 7RZ

t: 01538 300 401
f: 01538 300 585

title
David Beard and
Friends

medium
Acrylics on canvas

purpose of work
Promotional for the
client

brief
Paint a picture of
the reception area
to hang in the
reception area

commissioned by
Mark Wickens

company
Wickens Tutt
Southgate

lizzie harper

Top floor flat
11 Ullet Road
Liverpool
L17 3BP

t: 0151 733 5209

Small Tortoiseshell (*Aglais urticae*)
on foodplant Nettle. (*Urtica dioica*).

title
Tortoise-shell
Butterfly Life Cycle

medium
Watercolour and
gouache

purpose of work
Personal study of
insect life cycles in
the Yorkshire Dales

brief
To draw all life
cycle stages and
host plant in one
integrated image

kira josey

1 Vicarage Crescent
London
SW11 3LP

t: 0171 228 8882

title	**commissioned by**
Wadworth Map	Mike Thrasher
medium	**company**
Watercolour	Michael Stewart
purpose of work	Design Ltd
Brochure	**client**
brief	Wadworth & Co Ltd
To produce a map	**agent**
of Southwest	Illustration
England showing	1 Vicarage Crescent
the location of	London
Wadworth Public	SW11 3LP
Houses within the	t: 0171 228 8882
Wadworth Estate	

rachel marsh

Oronsay, Weintend
Great Urswick
Ulverston
Cumbria
LA12 0SS

t: 01229 587 888

title
Rabbit Dissection
medium
Watercolour and
gouache
purpose of work
College brief

brief
Produce a
professional
illustration of your
choice within four
weeks
agent
Blackpool College
of Art and Design

tilly northedge

10 Barley Mow
Passage
London
W4 4PH

t: 0181 994 6477
f: 0181 995 3049

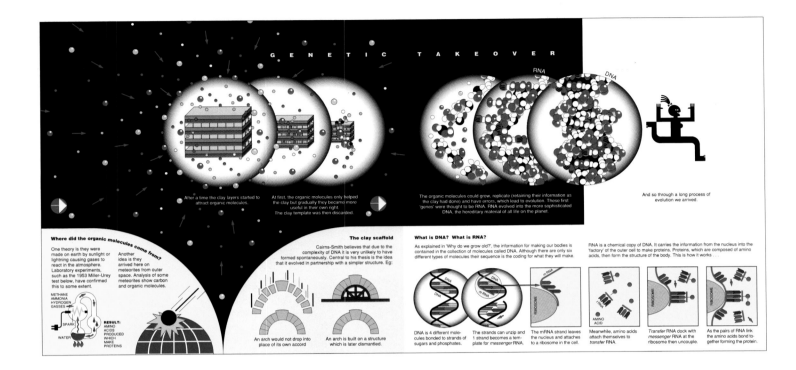

GENETIC TAKEOVER

After a time the clay layers started to attract organic molecules.

At first, the organic molecules only helped the clay but gradually they became more useful in their own right. The clay template was then discarded.

The organic molecules could grow, replicate (retaining their information as the clay had done) and have errors, which lead to evolution. These first 'genes' were thought to be RNA. RNA evolved into the more sophisticated DNA, the hereditary material of all life on the planet.

And so through a long process of evolution we arrived.

Where did the organic molecules come from?

One theory is they were made on earth by sunlight or lightning causing gases to react in the atmosphere. Laboratory experiments, such as the 1953 Miller-Urey test below, have confirmed this to some extent.

Another idea is they arrived here on meteorites from outer space. Analysis of some meteorites show carbon and organic molecules.

METHANE
AMMONIA
HYDROGEN
GASSES

SPARK

WATER

RESULT:
AMINO
ACIDS
PRODUCED
WHICH
MAKE
PROTEINS

The clay scaffold

Cairns-Smith believes that due to the complexity of DNA it is very unlikely to have formed spontaneously. Central to his thesis is the idea that it evolved in partnership with a simpler structure. Eg:

An arch would not drop into place of its own accord

An arch is built on a structure which is later dismantled.

What is DNA? What is RNA?

As explained in 'Why do we grow old?', the information for making our bodies is contained in the collection of molecules called DNA. Although there are only six different types of molecules their sequence is the coding for what they will make.

RNA is a chemical copy of DNA. It carries the information from the nucleus into the factory of the outer cell to make proteins. Proteins, which are composed of amino acids, then form the structure of the body. This is how it works . . .

DNA is 4 different molecules bonded to strands of sugars and phosphates.

The strands can unzip and 1 strand becomes a template for *messenger* RNA.

The mRNA strand leaves the nucleus and attaches to a ribosome in the cell.

Meanwhile, amino acids attach themselves to transfer RNA.

Transfer RNA dock with *messenger* RNA at the ribosome then uncouple.

As the pairs of RNA link the amino acids bond together forming the protein.

title	brief
How Did Life Begin? - 3	A self-set brief to research and explain a theory of how life began and also to learn computer skills
medium	
Computer	
purpose of work	
Self promotion	

ian james parker

Ceilidh
Coldharbour
Lingfield
RH7 6BZ

t: 01342 833583

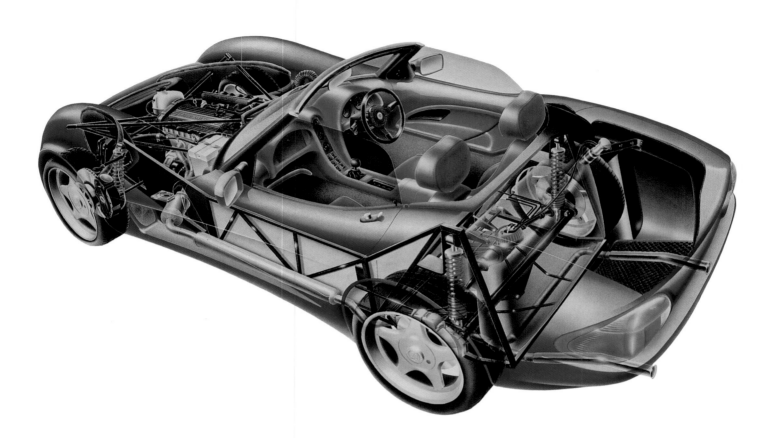

title
Caterham 21

medium
Watercolour

purpose of work
Self promotion

brief
To show the major
components in the
new Caterham
sports car

sally pinhey

664 Dorchester
Road
Upwey
DT3 5LE

t: 01305 813307
f: 01305 813307

title	brief
Beurre Diel, Beurre Hardy, Beurre Superfin and Black Worcester Pears	Watercolour paintings of 55 varieties of pears with leaves, cross-sections and some blossoms. Fifteen pages in all, three or four images to a page
medium	
Watercolour	
purpose of work	**commissioned by**
Illustrations for 'Pears', a book by Jim Arbury	Wells and Winter
	client
	Sir John Wells

lisa alderson
BLACKPOOL COLLEGE OF ART & DESIGN

294 Lowerhouse Lane
Burnley
BB12 6LZ
t: 01282 775371

title
Rooster Dissection

medium
Watercolour

purpose of work
College brief

brief
To clearly
demonstrate the
digestive track and
internal structure of
the rooster

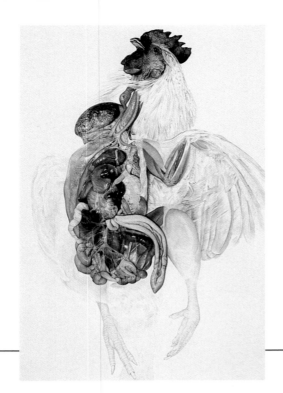

stuart ireland
BLACKPOOL COLLEGE OF ART & DESIGN

174 Hoghton Lane
Higher Walton
Preston
Lancashire
t: 01254 853 884

title
A still-life study of
exotic fruits

medium
Watercolour

purpose of work
College brief

brief
A professional brief to
illustrate a commercial
still life, studying
colour, form and
texture

simon mendez
BLACKPOOL COLLEGE OF ART & DESIGN

Viewlands
227 Malton Road
York, Yorkshire
Y03 9TD
t: 01904 421385

title
Barn Owl

medium
Mixed media

purpose of work
College brief

brief
To produce an image
of wildlife that is
aesthetically pleasing

☆ *images 22* exhibitor

lena kristensen
BLACKPOOL COLLEGE OF ART & DESIGN

Lundevej 56
Tune 4000 Roskilde
Denmark

t: 0045 46139354

137

GB

title
Amaryllis - Growth Habit

medium
Watercolour and gouache

purpose of work
Double page book spread

brief
Final year BA Hons design degree examination project

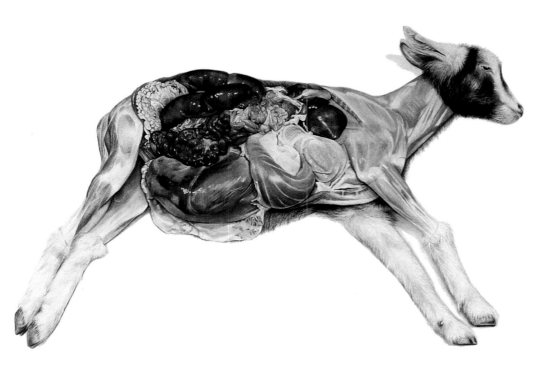

title
The Digestive System of Ruminants

medium
Gouache

purpose of work
Interpretative board for Blackpool Zoo

brief
To illustrate the digestive system of ruminants

print & design

Jane Ryan / Design Manager / Royal Mail

David Pearce / Managing Director / Tatham Pearce Design

Paul Leith / Illustrator

Andrew King / Creative Director / Landor Associates

Susan Buchanan / Partner / Buchanan-Davey

satoshi kambayashi

Flat 2
40 Tisbury Road
Hove
East Sussex
BN3 3BA

t: 01273 771539
f: 01273 771539
pager: 01426 131519

140
GB

title
Summersault/July

medium
India ink and
watercolour

purpose of work
Calendar

brief
Produce an
illustration for July
in the corporate
calendar

commissioned by
Setsuko Ikeda

company
Direct Image

agent
Ian Fleming and
Associates
72-74 Brewer
Street, London
W1R 3PH
t: 0171 734 8701

lesley buckingham

c/- CIA
36 Wellington
Street
London
WC2E 7BD

t: 0171 240 8925
f: 0171 836 1177

title	**brief**
A Floral	Valentine's
medium	packaging
Acrylic	**commissioned by**
purpose of work	Phil Cleever et al
In-house card	**client**
	Phil Cleever
	agency
	CIA
	36 Wellington
	Street
	London
	WC2E 7BD
	t: 0171 240 8925

rowan barnes-murphy

Crossing Cottage
North Charford
Fordingbridge
Hants
SP6 2DS

t: 01725 512 774
f: 01725 512 759

title
Savoy Gala
Invitation

medium
Pen, ink,
watercolour, crayon

purpose of work
Charity 'do'

brief
Re-use suitable
characters to
amuse in a stylistic
way

commissioned by
Frances Roach

company
Buckmans

client
The Douglas
Llambias Group of
Companies

rowan barnes-murphy

Crossing Cottage
North Charford
Fordingbridge
Hants
SP6 2DS

t: 01725 512 774
f: 01725 512 759

GB

title
All About
Performance and
Development

medium
Pen, ink,
watercolour, crayon

purpose of work
Bexley Heath
brochure

brief
"Before" and
"After" cartoons
hinting at the
benfits of a new
management
development
scheme

commissioned by
Alex Fea
TMP Worldwide

title
All About
Performance and
Development

medium
Pen, ink,
watercolour, crayon

purpose of work
Bexley Heath
brochure

brief
"Before" and
"After" cartoons
hinting at the
benfits of a new
management
development
scheme

commissioned by
Alex Fea
TMP Worldwide

marion deuchars

c/- Heart
1 Tysoe Street
London
EC1R 4SA

t: 0171 833 4447
f: 0171 833 4446

title
Brands and
Products

medium
Gouache

purpose of work
Illustrate an article
in "The Atticus
File"

brief
Depict the notion
that products exist
in reality, brands
only exist in the
minds of the
consumer

commissioned by
David Freeman

company
Sampson Tyrrell

agency
Heart
1 Tysoe Street
London
EC1R 4SA
t: 0171 833 4447

nelly dimitranova

Rat Corner
Top Flat, 33
Savernake Road
London
NW3 2JU

t: 0171 284 2334
f: 0171 284 2334

title
The Building
medium
Ink (brush)
purpose of work
Promotional page
for calendar

brief
To capture the
working
atmosphere of
Wood & Wood
Make Signs

commissioned by
John Wood

company
Wood & Wood
Make Signs

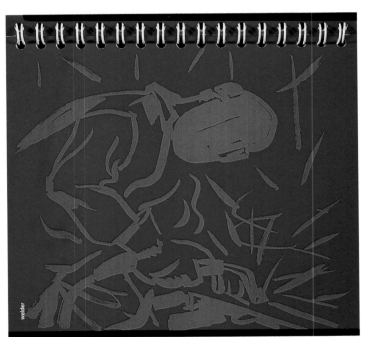

title
Welder
medium
Ink (brush)
purpose of work
Promotional page
for calendar

brief
To capture the
working
atmosphere of
Wood & Wood
Make Signs

commissioned by
John Wood

company
Wood & Wood
Make Signs

title
Reception
medium
Ink (brush)
purpose of work
Promotional page
for calendar

brief
To capture the
working
atmosphere of
Wood & Wood
Make Signs

commissioned by
John Wood

company
Wood & Wood
Make Signs

melvyn evans

c/- Catherine
Graham
Marks and Spencer
46-47 Baker Street
London W1

t: 0171 268 3386

title
Rice Packaging

medium
Lino cut

purpose of work
Part of the
packaging design

brief
To create strong
bold packaging
suitable for the
flexo print process
whilst reflecting the
country of origin of
the rice

commissioned by
Catherine Graham

company
Marks and Spencer

agent
New Division
32 Shelton Street
London
WC2H 9HP
t: 0171 497 2555

madeleine floyd

5 Beaumont
Crescent
London
W14 9LX

t: 0171 610 2381
f: 0171 610 2381

title
Bird Wrap

medium
Ink, watercolour

purpose of work
Wrapping paper

brief
To design a bird wrapping paper to accompany a range of 12 greetings cards

commissioned by
Art Angels Publishers

lara harwood

c/o Heart
2nd Floor
1 Tysoe Street
London EC1R 4SA

t: 0171 833 4447
f: 0171 833 4446

title
Communications
medium
Watercolour
purpose of work
Brochure

brief
One of a series of six for a firm of solicitors. This illustration is about internal communications within the different faculties of the firm - whereby the right arm knows what the left arm is doing so to speak.
commissioned by
Sue Howell
company
Fishburn Hedges
client
Osborne Clarke
agent
Heart
2nd Floor
1 Tysoe Street
London EC1R 4SA
t: 0171 833 4447
f: 0171 833 4446

lara harwood

c/o Heart
2nd Floor
1 Tysoe Street
London EC1R 4SA

t: 0171 833 4447
f: 0171 833 4446

title
Tools

medium
Watercolour

purpose of work
Brochure

brief
One of a series of
six for a firm of
solicitors. This
illustration deals
with the legal
'specialisms'
offered by the firm,
the idea stemming
from a Swiss army
knife

commissioned by
Sue Howell

company
Fishburn Hedges

client
Osborne Clarke

agent
Heart
2nd Floor
1 Tysoe Street
London EC1
t: 0171 833 4447

title
Relationships

medium
Watercolour

purpose of work
Brochure

brief
One of a series of
six for a firm of
solicitors. This
illustration relates
to the positive
relationship and
good
communication
skills that exist
between Osborne
Clarke and their
clients

commissioned by
Sue Howell

company
Fishburn Hedges

agent
Heart
2nd Floor
1 Tysoe Street
London EC1R 4SA
t: 0171 833 4447
f: 0171 833 4446

sara hayward

31 Diglis Road
Worcester
WR5 3BW

t: 01905 357 563
f: 01905 357 563

title
Pop Art
medium
Watercolour and
coloured pencil
purpose of work
Postcard
illustration

brief
To promote the
Whitbread's Pub
'Art Wimpenny's' in
Leeds
commissioned by
Mark Currie
company
Brahm Agency
client
Whitbread

sara hayward

31 Diglis Road
Worcester
WR5 3BW

t: 01905 357 563
f: 01905 357 563

title
Art Nouveau

medium
Watercolour and
coloured pencil

purpose of work
Postcard
illustration

brief
To promote the
Whitbread's Pub
'Art Wimpenny's'
in Leeds

commissioned by
Mark Currie

company
Brahm Agency

client
Whitbread

brian grimwood

36 Wellington St
London
WC2E 7BD

t: 0171 240 8925
f: 0171 836 1177

152
GB

title
The Faun

medium
Gouache

purpose of work
T-shirt design

brief
A T-shirt design

commissioned by
Cream Tea Limited

agent
CIA
36 Wellington
Street
London
WC2E 7BD
t: 0171 240 8925
email:
c.illustrationa@
dail.pipex.com

bruce ingman

c/- Heart
1 Tysoe Street
London
EC1R 4SA

t: 0171 833 4447
f: 0171 833 4446

title
Understanding the
Client Brief

medium
Gouache - collage

purpose of work
Illustrate article in
'The Atticus File'

brief
A better
understanding of
the client brief

commissioned by
David Freeman

company
Sampson Tyrrell

client
WPP Group plc

commissioned by
David Freeman

satoshi kambayashi

Flat 2
40 Tisbury Road
Hove
East Sussex
BN3 3BA

t: 01273 771539
f: 01273 771539
pager: 01426 131519

title
Children's Event

medium
India ink and
watercolour

purpose of work
South Bank
brochure/calendar

brief
Produce an
illustration for
Children's Events
section of South
Bank Centre's
calendar

commissioned by
John Pasche,
Paul Rollo

company
Royal Festival Hall

agent
Ian Fleming and
Associates
72-74 Brewer
Street, London
W1R 3PH
t: 0171 734 8701

patrick macallister

15 Lauderdale
House
Gosling Way
London
SW9 6JS

t: 0171 582 3344
f: 0171 582 3344

title
The Economic
Forecast Predicts
Choppy Waters
Ahead

medium
Crayon, watercolour

purpose of work
Quarterly report

brief
To convey the 'ups
and downs' of the
economic markets,
incorporating a
globe

commissioned by
Beatrice Maechler

company
Frontpage AG

client
Swiss Banking
Corporation

agent
Vetlibergstrasse 132
CH-8045 Zurich
Switzerland
t: 41 1-45753 13

clare mackie

21A Ursula Street
London
SW11 3DW

t: 0171 223 8649
f: 0171 223 8649

156
GB

title
The New Arrival
medium
Watercolour and
ink
purpose of work
Greetings card

brief
To create a 'New
Baby' card
commissioned by
Katherine Pierce
company
Graphique de
France

title
The Christmas Tree
medium
Watercolour and
ink
purpose of work
Cover for Christmas
catalogue

brief
To design a cover
for the 1996
Neiman Marcus
Christmas
catalogue
commissioned by
Eddie Nunns
company
Neiman Marcus

title
The Jester
medium
Watercolour and
ink
purpose of work
Greetings card

brief
To create a
Valentine's card
commissioned by
Katherine Pierce
company
Graphique de
France
agent
Eileen McMahon
and Co
PO Box 1062
Bayonne
New Jersey
07002
USA
t: 001 201 436 4362

james marsh

James Marsh
21 Elms Road
London
SW4 9ER

t: 0171 622 9530
f: 0171 498 6851

title
Looking Forward -
Looking Back
medium
Acrylic on canvas
purpose of work
Annual report -
cover

brief
To produce an
image around the
title for a 1996
report
commissioned by
Chris Passehl
company
Passehl Design
client
Orion Insurance
Company

title
Interactivity
medium
Acrylic on canvas
purpose of work
Annual report

brief
One of six images
for 1996 report -
illustration to fit
with title and text
commissioned by
Chris Passehl
company
Passehl Design
client
Orion Insurance
Company

title
Communication
medium
Acrylic on canvas
purpose of work
Annual report

brief
One of six images
for 1996 report -
illustration to fit
with title and text
commissioned by
Chris Passehl
company
Passehl Design
client
Orion Insurance
Company

ed bryant

c/- Central
Illustration Agency
36 Wellington
Street
London WC2E 7BD

t: 0171 240 8925
f: 0171 836 1177

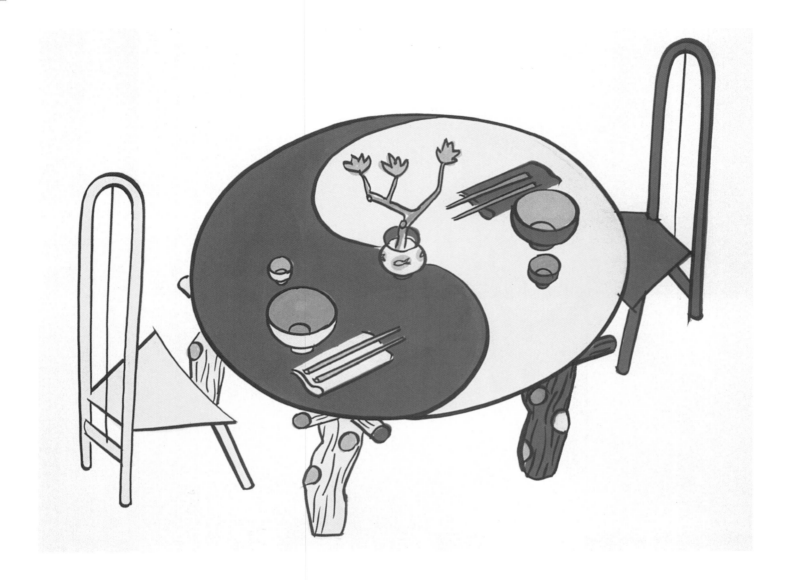

title
Yin-Yang Table

medium
Gouache

purpose of work
Illustrate article in
'The Atticus File'

brief
Observing cultural
traditions and
protocol when
working in China

commissioned by
David Freeman
Creative Director

company
Sampson Tyrrell

client
WPP Group plc

julie monks

42 Fenwick Road
East Dulwich
London
SE15 4HW

t: 0171 252 9243
f: 0171 252 9243

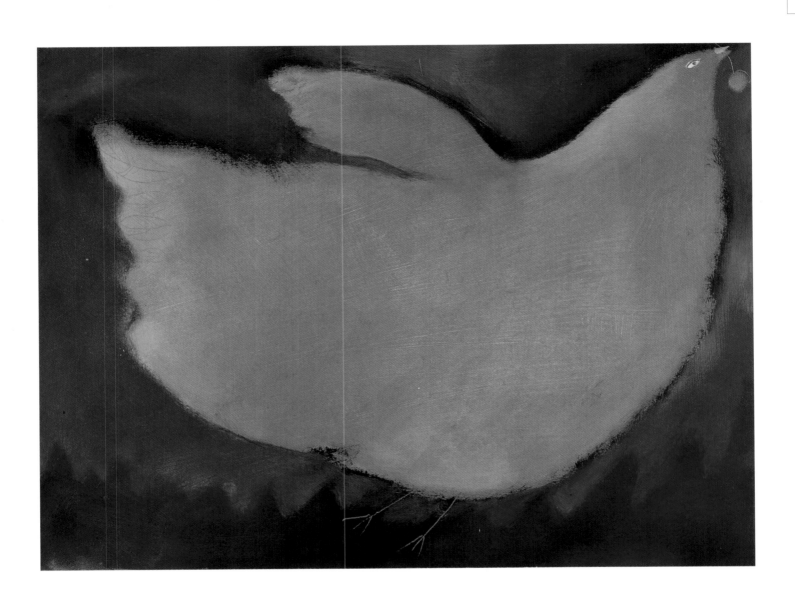

title
The Golden Bird

medium
Oil on paper

purpose of work
Greetings card
design

brief
Design a range of
eight greetings
cards

commissioned by
Jodi Ferris

company
Portico Designs Ltd

agent
Peters, Fraser &
Dunlop
503/4 The
Chambers
Chelsea Harbour
London SW10 0XF
t: 0171 344 1032

ian pollock

14 Crompton Road
Macclesfield
SK11 8DS

t: 01625 426 205
f: 01625 261 390

title
Hound of the
Baskervilles

medium
Watercolour inks,
Gouache

purpose of work
Postage stamp

brief
Postage stamp
designs for the
'Tales of Terror' set
issued by The
Royal Mail

commissioned by
The Royal Mail

company
The Royal Mail
Design Division

agent
The Inkshed
98 Columbia Road
London
E2 7QB
t: 0171 613 2323

paul powis

31 Diglis Road
Worcester
WR5 3BW

t: 01905 357 563
f: 01905 357 563

161

GB

title
Kalimera

medium
Acrylic

purpose of work
Packaging for
Greek food

brief
To produce an arid
landscape with a
high horizon,
strong shadows
and warm colours

commissioned by
Phil Carter

company
Carter Wong

client
Cypressa

petula stone

c/o Illustration
1 Vicarage Crescent
London
SW11 3LP

t: 0171 228 8882

title
Watermelon
medium
Watercolour, pencil
and coloured
pencils
purpose of work
Greetings card

brief
To produce four
cards with a
'botanical
notebook' feel
commissioned by
Louise Tighe
company
Paperlink Ltd
agent
Illustration
1 Vicarage Crescent
London
SW11 3LP
t: 0171 228 8882

title
Pomegranite
medium
Watercolour, pencil
and coloured
pencils
purpose of work
Greetings card

brief
To produce four
cards with a
'botanical
notebook' feel
commissioned by
Louise Tighe
company
Paperlink Ltd
agent
Illustration
1 Vicarage Crescent
London
SW11 3LP
t: 0171 228 8882

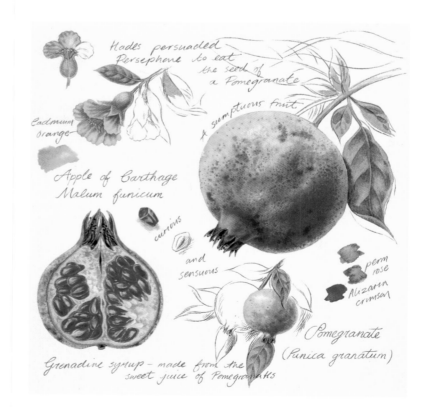

michael terry

12 Bartholomew
Street
Hythe
CT21 5BS

t: 01303 269 456
f: 01303 269 456

title
The White Lion
medium
Gouache and
coloured pencil
purpose of work
Inn sign for Bass
Taverns

brief
To humourously
illustrate the name
'The White Lion'
commissioned by
Mike Tisdale
company
Sign Specialists Ltd
client
Bass Taverns

title
Castell Mynach
medium
Gouache and
coloured pencil
purpose of work
Inn sign for Bass
Taverns

brief
To humourously
illustrate the Welsh
name which means
'Monk's Castle'
commissioned by
Richard Yarrell
company
Charby and Co Ltd
client
Bass Taverns

blaise thompson

c/- Heart
1 Tysoe Street
London
EC1R 4SA

t: 0171 833 4447
f: 0171 833 4446

title
Tribal Customs
medium
Gouache, collage
purpose of work
Illustrate article in
'The Atticus File'

brief
Depict the notion
of brands as
'badges' that cross
cultural and
geographical
barriers
commissioned by
David Freeman
company
Sampson Tyrrell
client
WPP Group plc
agent
Heart
1 Tysoe Street
London
EC1R 4SA
t: 0171 833 4447

peter warner

Peter Warner's Studio
Hillside Road
Tatsfield
Kent
TN16 2NH
England

p: 01959 577270
f: 01959 541414
mobile: 0958 531538

165

GB

title
Kitekat Leaping Cat

medium
Watercolour

purpose of work
Pet food packaging
for Europe

brief
To refine and make
more friendly the
rather vicious,
stuffed version (not
by me) of the
leaping cat I
created in 1987

commissioned by
Sylvia Vitale Rotta

company
Team Créatif

client
Mars Group Europe

peter warner

166
GB

Peter Warner's Studio
Hillside Road
Tatsfield
Kent
TN16 2NH
England

p: 01959 577270
f: 01959 541 414
mobile: 0958 531538

☆ *images 22* exhibitor

title
Whiskas Standing
Cat
medium
Watercolour
purpose of work
Pet food packaging
for Europe

brief
To 'modernise' my
1987 cat, making
him young,
debonair, gay,
happy, healthy,
active, dynamic
and loving, using
body language and
a narrow pose
commissioned by
Sylvia Vitale Rotta
company
Team Créatif
client
Mars Group Europe

peter warner

Peter Warner's Studio
Hillside Road
Tatsfield
Kent
TN16 2NH
England

p: 01959 577270
f: 01959 541414
mobile: 0958 531538

167

GB

title
Whiskas Advance
Adult Cat
medium
Watercolour
purpose of work
Veterinary pet food
packaging

brief
One of four
interrelated
illustrations to
depict different age
groups catered for
by specialised dry
food.
commissioned by
Sylvia Vitale Rotta
company
Team Créatif
client
Mars Group Europe

ian whadcock

c/- Sampson Tyrrell
6 Mercer Street
London
WC2H 9QA

t: 01625 618 068

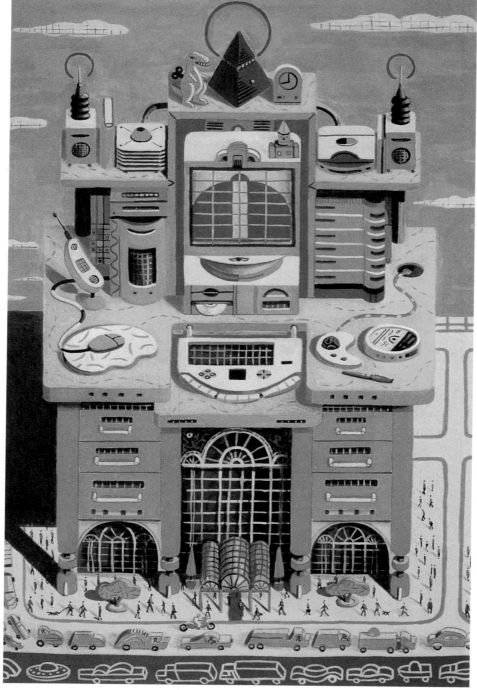

title
The Office Hotel
medium
Gouache
purpose of work
Illustrate article in
'The Atticus File'

brief
Depict the concept
of the office as
hotel
commissioned by
David Freeman
company
Sampson Tyrrell
client
WPP Group plc

susan wintringham

50 Troutbeck Road
Gatley
Cheadle
Cheshire
SK8 4RR
t/f: 0161 428 5727
mobile: 0973 715 617

title	**brief**
Bengal Tiger	Greetings card
medium	**commissioned by**
Monoprint	Pieter Kwant
purpose of work	**company**
Greetings card	Paternoster
	Publishing

unpublished

unpublished professional
judges

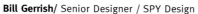

GB

Bill Gerrish/ Senior Designer / SPY Design

Ian Pollock / Illustrator & AOI Patron

Genevieve Webster / Art Director / Children's Books, Reed Publishing

Tamlyn Hennessey / Artist's Representative / Arena

Debi Angel / Art Director / *Elle Decoration*

neil breeden

28 Vere Road
Brighton
BN1 4NR

t: 01273 700 857

★ unpublished section winner
☆ *images 22* exhibitor

title
A Revolution is not
a Dinner Party

medium
Acrylic on wood

purpose of work
Self promotion

brief
To illustrate a
political
comparison
between
Robespierre and
Chairman Mao

john bates

27 Faraday Road
Welling
Kent
DA16 2ET

t: 0181 304 0707

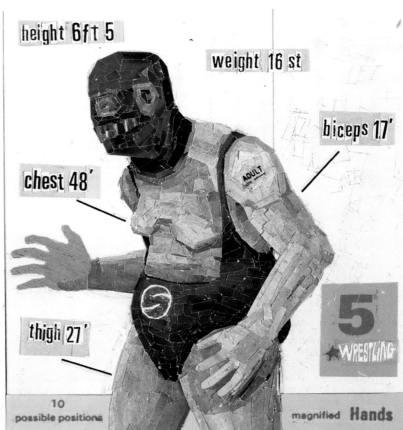

title
Wrestlemaniac

medium
Collage

purpose of work
Personal promotion

brief
You are what you eat (views on popular consumerism)

c/- Folio
10 Gate Street
London
WC2A 3HP

t: 0171 242 9562

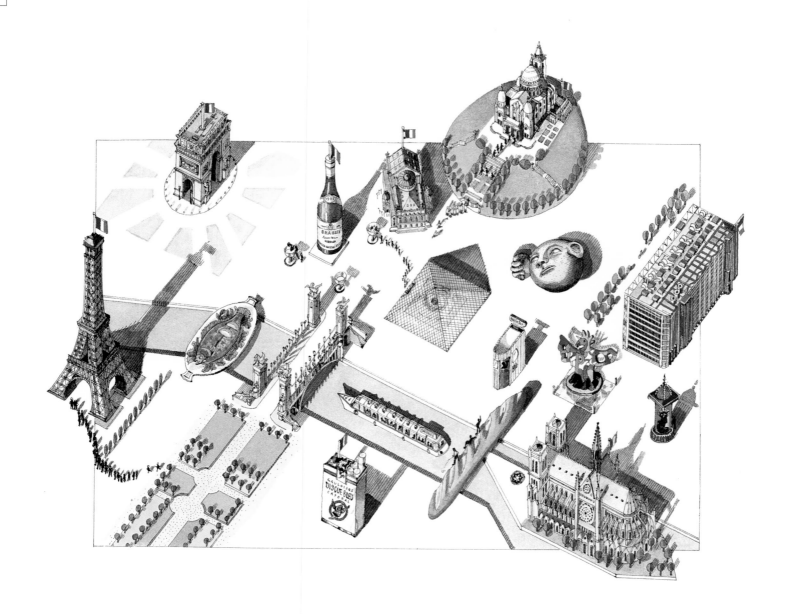

title	brief
Paris	Specimen/
medium	promotional
Watercolour, pen	**agency**
and ink	Folio
purpose of work	10 Gate Street
Specimen/	London
promotional	WC2A 3HP
	t: 0171 242 9562

michael bramman

104 Dudley Court
Upper Berkeley St
London
W1H 7PJ

t: 0171 723 3564
f: 0171 723 3564

GB

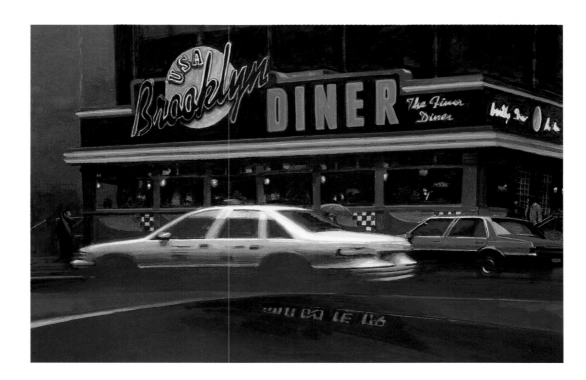

title
Brooklyn
medium
Acrylic
purpose of work
Self promotion
brief
Self promotion

title
Broadway Bunny
medium
Acrylic
purpose of work
Self promotion
brief
Self promotion

neil breeden

28 Vere Road
Brighton
BN1 4NR

t: 01273 700 857

title
Landing

medium
Acrylic on wood

purpose of work
Self promotion

brief
To illustrate a children's story on the theme of flying fish

michael charsley

EPSOM SCHOOL OF ART & DESIGN

17 Felbridge Close
Sutton
Surrey
SM2 5QH

t: 0181 642 2922

title
The Stones

medium
Airbrush, oils

purpose of work
Self promotional

brief
Self promotional

agent
Ms Michele
Robinson
t: 0181 642 1170

janie coath

c/o Illustration
1 Vicarage Crescent
London
SW11 3LP

t: 0171 228 8882

title
Magic Horse

medium
Acrylic and oil
pastel

purpose of work
Piece from a recent
exhibition

brief
Exhibition theme
'Pantomime Angels'

agency
Illustration
1 Vicarage Crescent
London
SW11 3LP
t: 0171 228 8882

louise denning

41 Goddard Way
Saffron
Walden
CB10 2DQ

t: 01799 513387

title
The Man who
Planted Trees - 2
medium
Charcoal
purpose of work
Interior illustration
for book
brief
To illustrate the
story of the same
name

title
The Man who
Planted Trees - 3
medium
Pastel
purpose of work
Book cover
brief
Book cover to
illustrate the story
of the same name

max ellis

8 Elfin Lodge
Elfin Grove
Teddington
TW11 8RE

t/f: 0181 977 8924

title
Phutur Bitch
medium
Digitally-sampled
montage
purpose of work
Promotion for the
club The Ministry of
Sound

brief
Respond to the
theme "Phutur
(Future) Bitch"
commissioned by
Will Harvey
client
Ministry of Sound

pete ellis

118 Northborough
Road
Norbury
London
SW16 4AZ

t: 0181 764 0394
f: 0181 764 0394

title
Ladies Who Lunch
medium
Ink
purpose of work
Self promotional

brief
To produce a series
of black and white
spot illustrations
on holidays

emma garner

The Craft and
Design Centre
6 Leonard Lane
Bristol BS1 1EA
t: 0976 410171
f: 0117 929 7890

182
GB

title
Alphabet
medium
Mixed media
purpose of work
Personal project

brief
Speculative
giftwrap/poster
design

caroline glicksman

Geitmyrsveien 31B
N-0171 Oslo
Norway
t: 0047 911 36 656
f: 0047 22696363
(from Aug '98
contact AOI
p: 0171 831 7377
f: 0171 831 6277
for new UK details)

And finding she was left alone,
Went tiptoe to the Telephone

And summoned the Immediate Aid
Of London's Noble Fire-Brigade.

title
And finding she
was left alone....
medium
Hand-coloured
drawing
purpose of work
Self-promotional
artist's book

brief
Illustrate Hilaire
Belloc's cautionary
tale 'Matilda'

elena gomez

Stonelands
Portsmouth Road
Milford
Godalming
GU8 5DR

t: 01483 423 876
f: 01483 423 935

☆ *images 22* exhibitor

title
Four Orchard Geese

medium
Acrylic

purpose of work
Self promotional

brief
Self promotional

maxine hall

1 Vicarage Crescent
London
SW11 3LP

t: 0171 228 8882 /
   01332 203 909
f: 01332 203 909

title
Mad Cow Disease

medium
Computer

purpose of work
Exhibition

brief
Self promotional

agent
Illustration
1 Vicarage Crescent
London
SW11 3LP
t: 0171 228 8882

robin harris

60 Weltje Road
London
W6 9LT

t: 0181 748 5998

title
The Fortune Teller

medium
Mixed

purpose of work
Illustrations for
Midnight's Children

brief
llustrations for
Midnight's Children
attempting to bring
my own personal
way of work to a
brief without it
dying of tightness

kevin hauff

7 Pendre Avenue
Prestatyn
LL19 9SH

t: 01745 888734
f: 01745 888734

title
Rocket Man

medium
Acrylic

purpose of work
Self promotion

brief
Image based upon
an optimistic quote
from the 1950s -
'Space travel will
soon be available
to the individual -
just strap on your
rocket and go!'

nick hersey

185a Victoria
Park Road
London
E9 7JN

t: 0181 525 5592

title
Fearful Iraq
medium
Acrylic
purpose of work
Editorial

brief
An editorial piece
illustrating the
persecution of
women in Iraq

james hill

4 Manor Road
Sole Street
Cobham
Kent
DA13 9BN

t: 01474 814680

title
Nova Express

medium
Digital print

purpose of work
Speculative project
directed at
publishers

brief
Reflect the novel's
sci-fi sympathies
without resort to
martian/monster
imagery

david hitch

c/- Arena
144 Royal College
Street
London
NW1 0TA

t: 0171 267 9661
f: 0171 284 0486

☆ *images 22* exhibitor

190
GB

title
Christmas
medium
Acrylic
purpose of work
Speculative

brief
Sample piece done
for possible
packaging for
Marks and Spencer

david hitch

c/- Arena
144 Royal College
Street
London
NW1 0TA

t: 0171 267 9661
f: 0171 284 0486

GB

title
Hallowe'en

medium
Acrylic

purpose of work
Speculative

brief
Sample piece done
for possible
packaging for
Marks and Spencer

agent
Arena
144 Royal College
Street
London
NW1 0TA
t: 0171 267 9661

roger hulley

46 The Avenue
Ealing
London
W13 8LR

t: 0181 997 5003
f: 0181 997 5003

★ **award winner:** *The Daler Rowney Award*
☆ *images 22* exhibitor

title
Beware of false
prophets who come
in sheep's clothing
NE: 14:15

medium
Acrylics and oils

purpose of work
Self promotion

brief
Visually interpret a
phrase form the
Book of Mormon

title
Those who possess
land of promise
must serve God or
be swept off
ETHER 2:8

medium
Acrylics and oils

purpose of work
Self promotion

brief
Visually interpret a
phrase form the
Book of Mormon

commissioned by
Ian Miller/The CW
Daniel Company
Limited

warwick johnson-cadwell Eastwing
98 Columbia Road
London
E2 7QB

t: 0171 613 5580

title
Amongst the Pod

medium
Acrylic, pastel

purpose of work
Self directed

brief
Illustration from
Moby Dick

henning löhlein

Bristol Craft and
Design Centre
6 Leonard Lane
Bristol
BS1 1EA

t: 0117 9299077
f: 0117 9299077

194
GB

title
The Queen

medium
Acrylic

purpose of work
Self promotional

brief
To design a stamp
to go with the
illustrator's
stationery

james marsh

21 Elms Road
London
SW4 9ER

t: 0171 622 9530
f: 0171 498 6851

title
Brighter Futures
medium
Acrylic on canvas
purpose of work
Magazine DPS
brief
To illustrate an
article about future
stock investments
commissioned by
Rudy Hoglund
company
Money Magazine

title
Wet Dream
medium
Acrylic on canvas
purpose of work
Gallery work
brief
One in a series of
self-generated
images with a sea
theme

belle mellor

The Old Hall
Mulbarton
Norwich
Norfolk NR14 8JS

t: 01973 463942/01508 570241
f: 01508 578655

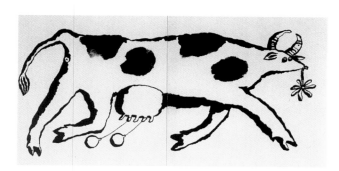

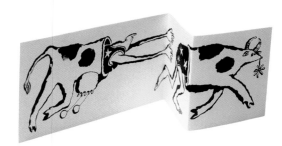

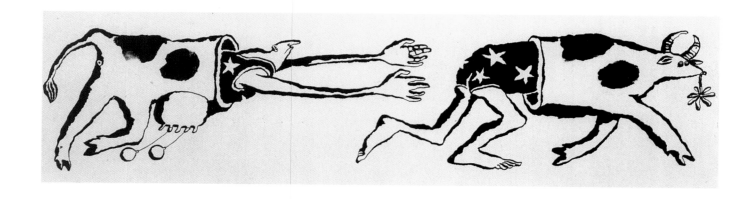

title
Cow

medium
Pen and ink

purpose of work
Christmas card for
self-promotion

brief
Self promotional

lydia monks

42 Fenwick Road
East Dulwich
London
SE15 4HW

t: 0171 639 8534
f: 0171 639 8534
mobile: 0973 908 301

title
The Suit

medium
Mixed

purpose of work
Self promotion

brief
'The Suit' is a poem taken from *Bad Bad Cats* by Roger McGough, which I originally illustrated in black and white

commissioned by
Ronnie Fairweather
Puffin

david smith

65 Breech Lane
Walton-on-the-Hill
Surrey KT20 7SJ

t: 01737 814 189
f: 01737 814 190

198
GB

title	**brief**
Body 8	Experimental
medium	**agent**
Collage	Eastwing
purpose of work	98 Columbia Road
Self initiated/	London
experimental	E2 7QB
	t: 0171 613 5580

tim stevens

Tim Stevens
40 Upper Park
Loughton
IG10 4EQ

t: 0181 508 1974

199
GB

title
Jack Spratt
medium
Pen and ink
purpose of work
Self promotion

brief
To illustrate the
nursery rhyme 'Jack
Spratt would eat
no fat, his wife
would eat no lean'

craig thomson

13 Close Street
Carlisle
CA1 2HB

t: 01228 596446

200
GB

title
Street Theatre

medium
Pen and ink,
computer

purpose of work
Self promotion of
new style

brief
Self-set project -
one of four images
produced to convey
different elements
of the Edinburgh
Festival

sarah wilkins

Flat H
Welbeck Mansions
Inglewood Road
London
NW6 1QX

t: 0171 431 8183
f: 0171 431 8183

title
ABC

medium
Acrylic

purpose of work
Self-promotional
poster

brief
Self-promotional
poster

agent
New Division
32 Shelton Street
London
WC2H 9JN
t: 0171 497 2555

title
Letters

medium
Acrylic

purpose of work
Personal promotion

brief
Personal promotion

david williams

c/o Arena
144 Royal College
Street
London
NW1 oTA

t: 0171 267 9661
f: 0171 284 0486

title
Angel Embrace
medium
Acrylic
purpose of work
Painting for Labour
Party offices at
Millbank

brief
Part of a body of
work privately
commissioned by
the Labour Party
commissioned by
The Labour Party
agent
Arena
144 Royal College
Street
London
NW1 oTA
t: 0171 267 9661

sue williams

c/- Folio
10 Gate Street
Lincoln's Inn Fields
London WC2A
3HP

t: 0171 242 9562

203

GB

title
Colman's Mustard
medium
Acrylic on canvas
purpose of work
Experimental work
with new medium,
culminating in the
exhibition: Still Life
- A Celebration

brief
Work inspired by
traditional still life,
using familiar
forms, utilities,
foods and
packaging
reconsidering these
mundane objects in
a new light

agent
Folio
10 Gate Street
Lincolns Inn Fields
London
WC2A 3HP
t: 0171 242 9562

title
Vita Ghee
medium
Acrylic on canvas
purpose of work
For the exhibition:
Still Life - A
Celebration

brief
Work inspired by
traditional still life,
using familiar
forms, utilities,
foods and
packaging
reconsidering these
mundane objects in
a new light

agent
Folio
10 Gate Street
Lincolns Inn Fields
London
WC2A 3HP
t: 0171 242 9562

student

Jonathan Christie / Senior Designer / *Radio Times*

Nancy Anderson / Illustrator

Sarah Odedina / Editorial Director / Bloomsbury Children's Books

John Belknap / Art Director / *The Express*

Anne Magill / Illustrator

adrian johnson
KINGSTON UNIVERSITY

3 Owen Mansions
Queen's Club
Gardens
London W14 9RS

t: 0171 381 2852
mobile: 0958 670750

206
GB

title
Tabasco, Sombrero, Bandido
medium
Acrylic and pencil on board
purpose of work
Self initiated for major project

brief
One of a series of illustrations based loosely on the subject of hats - this one being 'I'll eat my hat'

charlotte combe
WOLVERHAMPTON UNIVERSITY

8 Wolverley Road
Kidderminster
DY11 5JN

t: 01562 822358

207

GB

title
The Cat and the Cock

medium
Oil paint

purpose of work
Course work

brief
This illustration is for Aesop's fable called the *Cat and the Cock*

title
Coffee Shops in Amsterdam

medium
Oil paint

purpose of work
Course work

brief
This is an illustration to show life in Amsterdam's café bars for younger people, could be used for a guide book or editorial

louis xu zheng fu
CHELSEA COLLEGE OF ART

125 Champlain House
Canada Way
London
W12 7QW

t: 0181 749 2406
f: 0181 749 2406

title
From my Window 1

brief
self promotion

medium
Mixed media

purpose of work
Advertisement

title
From my Window 2

brief
self promotion

medium
Mixed media

purpose of work
Advertisement

title
From my Window 4

brief
self promotion

medium
Mixed media

purpose of work
Book cover

louis xu zheng fu
CHELSEA COLLEGE OF ART

125 Champlain
House
Canada Way
London
W12 7QW

t: 0181 749 2406
f: 0181 749 2406

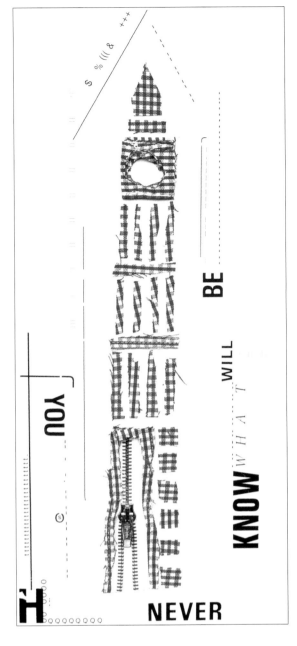

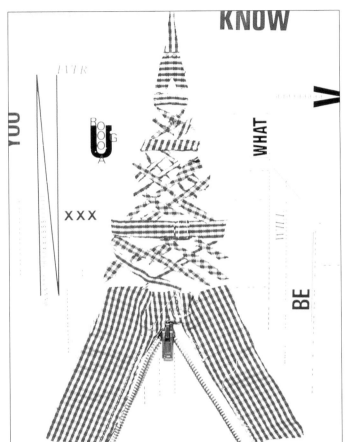

title
You Never Know
What Will Be 1&2
medium
Mixed media
purpose of work
Advertisement
brief
The illustrations
created could be
used for travel
agents

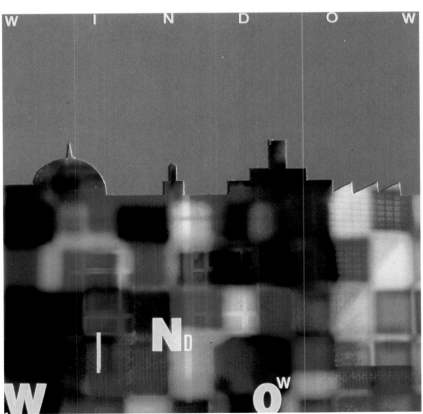

title   **brief**
From my Window 3   self promotion
medium
Mixed
purpose of work
CD or record cover

nicolette green
BRIGHTON UNIVERSITY

96 Stanford Avenue
Brighton
BN1 6FE

t: 01273 506 875
f: 01273 506 875
email: nickies@pavilion.co.uk

title
Fevronia and the Wolves

medium
Watercolours, gouache, bleach

purpose of work
MA project - 24-page picture book *Two Russian Tales*

brief
Full page illustration from *The Lost City of Kitezh* introducing Fevronia who is part madonna/part-witch and able to pacify the fiercest of animals

title
Sadko Sings at the Merchants' Banquet

medium
Lino cut

purpose of work
MA project, 24-page book *Two Russian Tales*

brief
First illustration for *Sadko and the Sea King* to evoke the style and feel of Russian 'Lubok' illustrations.

shahid mahmood
ANGLIA POLY UNIVERSITY

263 Clarence Road
Peterborough
PE1 2LH

t: 01733 558 716

title
Breakfast Hat

medium
Photocopier/black/
blue/red/green
toner

purpose of work
College project

brief
To produce a book
on alternative hats

mark preston
ANGLIA POLYTECHNIC UNIVERSITY

19 Albany Road
Derby
DE22 3LW

t: 01332 364 125

title
London Street at
Night

medium
Oil pastel

purpose of work
College brief

brief
To produce an
image based on
some aspect of
London life, for *ES
Magazine*

maria raymondsdotter
KINGSTON UNIVERSITY

c/o Kingston University
Knights Park
Kingston upon Thames
Surrey
KT1 2QJ

t: 0181 547 2000 ext: 4152

213

GB

title
Nice Barnet

medium
Acrylics

purpose of work
Editorial
illustration

brief
Article for
hairculture (for
exhibition)

tom sanderson

UNIVERSITY OF BRIGHTON

17 Wakefield Road
Brighton
BN2 3FP

t: 01273 389 484

title
Busy as a Bee

medium
Lino collage

purpose of work
Portfolio

brief
Illustrating an
article on business
people working
longer hours

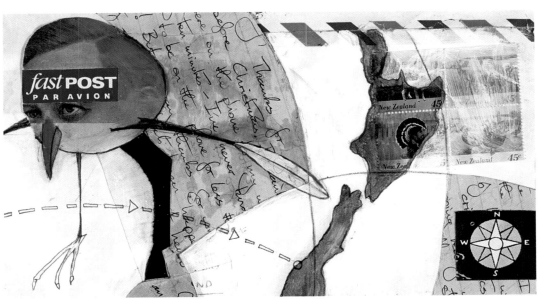

tom sanderson

UNIVERSITY OF BRIGHTON

17 Wakefield Road
Brighton
BN2 3FP

t: 01273 389 484

title
Japanese Kite
Fighting
medium
Lino, collage and
Photoshop
Purpose of work
For promotional
magazine
Brief
Illustrating an article
on Japanese kite
Fighting

kelly andrews

MIDDLESEX UNIVERSITY

2 Lessness Road
Off Stapley Road
Nuxley Village
Upper Belvedere
Kent
DA17 5JT

t: 01322 439 177

title
Air Mail
medium
Collage, oil paint,
graphite pencil
purpose of work
Illustration from a
series entitled
'Visual A to Z'
brief
To visually
illustrate selected
works,
alphabetically

zoe attwood

Lynward
4 Hunts Hill
Glemsford
Sudbury, Suffolk
CO10 7RL

t: 01787 281365

title
Commuter (A
Queen of Victoria)
medium
Pastel
purpose of work
Self promotion
brief
From a group of
drawings focusing
on the
personalities of
women passing
through Victoria
station, London

ariane beckman

CAMBERWELL COLLEGE OF ARTS

Odessaer-Str 24
16548 Glienicke
Berlin
Germany

t: 0177 2994424

title
The Scream
medium
Photography
(Black and White)
purpose
Personal
experimental work
for a photostory or
posters
brief
Black and white
photography as an
abstract medium
for subjective and
creative
interpretation of
body and feature

jonathan beech

UNIVERSITY OF CENTRAL LANCASTER

153 Kirkham Road
Freckleton
Near Preston
Lancs

t: 01772 633 957

title
Blue Surveillance
medium
Alkyds
purpose
Interior illustration
for *The New York
Trilogy* by Paul
Auster
brief
An image which
gives the viewer an
atmospheric insight
for the book *The
New York Trilogy*

johe beuker

UNIVERSITY OF BRIGHTON

Oakwell Studio
8 Vicarage Hill
Kingsteignton
S Devon
TQ12 3BA

t: 01626 61607

title
Cakey Cottage
medium
Mixed
purpose
Illustration to
Hansel and Gretel
brief
To develop pictures
based on fairy tales
(in this case *Hansel
and Gretel*) to
incorporate a maze
and hidden objects
for children to find

glyn brewerton

SWINDON COLLEGE

8 Apple Garth
Easingwold
York
YO6 3LZ

t: 01347 823 087
f: 01347 823 087

217

GB

title
Another Day
Wrapped Up

medium
Charcoal, conte
crayon

purpose of work
Major college
project

brief
Illustrate the hymn
Jerusalem by
William Blake,
depicting the 'dark
satanic mills' from
my own working
experience in a
factory
environment

scot burgoyne
UNIVERSITY OF THE WEST OF ENGLAND

82 Toronto Road
Horfield
Bristol
BS7 oJT

t: 0117 9692 821

218
GB

title
1909 - Those
Wright Brothers are
at it Again

medium
Watercolour,
gouache and pencil
crayon

purpose of work
Final degree show

brief
A self-directed
project, in which I
took a slightly
alternative view of
various historical
events

bérengère ducoms

MIDDLESEX UNIVERSITY

13 Eve Road
London
N17 6YD

t: 0181 493 0635

title	**brief**
Him	Transformation
medium	
Monoprint	
purpose of work	
Personal work	

lynn evans
LOUGHBOROUGH COLLEGE OF ART AND DESIGN

220
GB

110 Mobbsbury
Way
Stevenage
SG2 oJA

t: 01438 232475

title
Topiary
medium
Lino cut
purpose
College project
brief
Illustrate article
'Between the Lines'
on topiary in
British gardens

---

sarah louise godfrey
CENTRAL SAINT MARTINS

26 Mansfield Road
Hillstown
Chesterfield
S44 6LH

t: 01246 822997

title
Over the Rainbow
medium
Mixed
purpose
Personal project
brief
Produce a series
of images
inspired by the
writings of the
North American
Indians and how
they thought the
world was
created

---

peter gray
LOUGHBOROUGH COLLEGE OF ART AND DESIGN

19 Clapgate Drive
Little Clacton
CO16 9PP

t: 01255 860 946
f: 01255 860 534

title
Scale
medium
Acrylic
purpose
College project
brief
Book cover for
Scale by Will Self

lizzie harper

B.P.C.A.D.

title
Pygmy Hippo

medium
Acrylic

purpose of work
College brief

brief
To represent an
endangered species
in a habitat,
composition and
atmosphere
appropriate to it

Top floor flat
11 Ullet Road
Liverpool
L17 3BP

t: 0151 733 5209

---

neal layton

CENTRAL SAINT MARTIN'S

CHARACTERS
in order of appearance...

Dorothy and
Toto

Aunt Em

Uncle Henry

The Scarecrow

The Tin
Woodman

The Cowardly
Lion

title
Wizard of Oz:
The Characters

medium
Pencil, ink,
watercolour

purpose of work
Illustration for the
classic children's
text

brief
To design and
illustrate a page
showing the main
characters of the
text

181a Northcote
Battersea
London
SW11 6QF

Domanic Li

STOCKPORT COLLEGE

title
Family Doctor
Series

medium
Acrylic

purpose of work
College project

brief
To produce four
illustrations for the
Family Doctor
series of health
information books

483 Newtondale
Sutton Park Estate
Hull
HU7 4BW

t: 01482 820004

emily mitchell

CENTRAL SAINT MARTIN'S

3 Grove Mansions
Clapham Common
North Side
London
SW4 9SL

t: 0171 228 7496

title
The Bloody
Chamber

medium
Mixed

purpose
Book cover

brief
To produce a book
cover for Angela
Carter's *The Bloody
Chamber*, a re-
working of the
Bluebeard Story

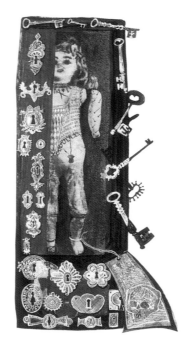

caroline osborne

FALMOUTH COLLEGE OF ARTS

The Rectory
Richmond Place
Lansdown
Bath
BA1 5PZ

t: 01225 317 535

title
Time's Arrow

medium
Mixed

purpose
Book cover

brief
To produce a book
cover for *Time's
Arrow* by Martin
Amis

david stevenson

LOUGHBOROUGH COLLEGE OF ART AND DESIGN

25 Itchen Grove
Perton
Wolverhampton
WV6 7QY

t: 01902 750 419

title
Cloudy Day

medium
Acrylic

purpose
Wine label

brief
Packaging for a
wine label

susy smith
UNIVERSITY OF BRIGHTON

7a Eaton Grove
Hove
East Sussex
BN3 3PH

t: 01273 207 953

223

GB

title
The House of the
Spirits - 1 & 2

purpose
Personal projects

medium
Acrylic on board

brief
Project to illllustrate
*The House of the
Spirits* by Isabel
Allende

ben warwick
LOUGHBOROUGH COLLEGE OF ART AND DESIGN

title
Hôtel Des
Commandeurs De
Saint. Jerusalem,
Pezenas, South
France

purpose
To capture the
enlightening spirit
of South France

medium
Pencil and
watercolour

brief
A personal
travelogue:
painting selected
from a series
produced on
location

58 High Street West
Uppingham
Rutland
LE15 9QD

t: 01572 822487
f: 01572 822487

stephen waterhouse
LOUGHBOROUGH COLLEGE OF ART AND DESIGN

2A Norwood Grove
Birkenshaw
Bradford
BD11 2NP

t: 01274 877 111

title
Building in Greece
medium
Acrylic
purpose
College project
brief
To show
simplification of
both colour and
mark

title
Loughborough
Balloon Festival
medium
Acrylic
purpose
College project
brief
Exercise in poster
design

sarah welch
SOMERSET COLLEGE OF ARTS AND TECHNOLOGY

Marsh Cottage
North Perrott Road
Misterton
Crewkerne
TA18 7SB

t: 01460 78931

title
Travelling
Exhibition Poster
medium
Tin, coloured paper
for background
purpose
Poster advertising
Paul Smith's
Travelling
Exhibition in
Blackpool
brief
Produce a
keepsake for Paul
Smith's Travelling
Exhibition in a
chosen city and
produce a poster

nicholas J williams

FALMOUTH COLLEGE OF ART

33 Chestnut Drive
Wanstead
London
E11 2TA

t: 0181 923 4875

title
Who Killed Cock
Robin

medium
Etching with
aquatint

purpose
book illustration

brief
Produce a set of 15
black and white
images, illustrating
a set of nursery
rhymes

☆ *images 22* exhibitor

samantha wilson

KINGSTON UNIVERSITY

Flat 1
45 Lovelace Road
Surbiton
Surrey
KT6 6NA

t: 0181 399 9651
f: 0181 873 1102

So straight away the brave little fella, not showing a morsel of fear,
Took his stick with his horses head handle and shoved it in Wallis' ear.

title
The Lion and
Albert: The Poking
Scene

medium
Screen print and
collage

purpose
Self initiated

brief
To illustrate the
story of the lion
and Albert by
Stanley Holloway
and Marriott Edgar

AOI membership benefits & costs

Membership of the AOI is open to all illustrators, illustration students, agents, lecturers and illustration clients.

All categories of membership receive the following benefits:

- Monthly journal
- Discounted rate at events
- Discounted rate for *Images* – call for entries, hanging fees and annual pages
- Access to professional practice workshops
- Contact details on office database for enquiries from clients
- Access to the portfolio insurance scheme
- Portfolio stickers
- Return of artwork stickers
- Discounts from material suppliers
- Regional group contacts

In addition we provide the following services for particular types of membership:–

Full Membership: £85

This category is for professional illustrators who have had work commissioned and accept the AOI code of conduct.

- Legal advice on contracts and book publishing agreements
- Hotline information on pricing and professional practice
- Free annual portfolio surgery
- Opportunity to use foyer exhibition space
- Reduced rated account with photographic services, couriers and printers
- Invitation to the *Images* private view
- Central London meeting place with clients
- Discounted rate on selected hotel accommodation in London
- Editorial and publishing directories
- Business advice – an hour's free consultation with a chartered accountant on accounts, book–keeping, National Insurance, VAT and tax
- Full members are entitled to use the affix 'Mem AOI'
- Full members are supplied with a list of agents and advice about agents

Associate Membership: £60

This one-year category is for newcomers and illustrators on their first year out of college who have not published work. In exceptional circumstances this membership can be extended.

- Hotline information on pricing and professional practice
- Free annual portfolio surgery
- Discounted rate on selected hotel accommodation in London
- Editorial and publishing directories
- Business advice – an hour's free consultation with a chartered accountant on accounts, book-keeping, National Insurance, VAT and tax.

Student membership: £40

This service is for students on full-time illustration or related courses

- See above services for all AOI members

Corporate Membership: £165

This service is for agents and clients from the illustration industry

- Free copy of the *Images* catalogue
- Invitation to the *Images* private view
- All corporate members' staff and illustrators will receive discounts on events and *Images*

Association of Illustrators

1st Floor, 32/38 Saffron Hill
London EC1N 8FH
Telephone: 0171 831 7377
Fax: 0171 831 6277

RONALD SEARLE

AOI publications

Rights: The Illustrator's Guide to Professional Practice

This is the only comprehensive guide to all aspects of the law specifically related to illustration. It includes model terms and conditions, information about copyright, contracts, book publishing agreements, agency agreements, advice about going to the law, how to calculate fees and guidance on how to write a licence.

Rights is the result of a number of years of research and is the only comprehensive guide to aspects of the law specifically related to the illustration business. It has been approved by solicitors and contains the most detailed and accurate model terms and conditions available for use by illustrators or clients.

Price: Non-members £25 + £1 p&p
AOI Members £15 + £1 p&p

Survive: The Illustrator's Guide to a Professional Career

This invaluable publication covers all aspects of the illustration business and is an indispensable guide to anyone wishing to embark on a professional career in illustration. Written by illustration experts, *Survive* covers a wide range of subjects including getting started, clients, agents, money, reference and technical information and ethics.

Price: Non-members £9 + £1 p&p
AOI Members £7 + £1 p&p

index